Fantastic Imaginary Creatures

An Anthology
of Contemporary
Prose Poems

For Carlo, who surely is fantastic

Fantastic Imaginary Creatures

An Anthology of Contemporary Prose Poems

edited by
Gerry LaFemina

MADVILLE
PUBLISHING

LAKE DALLAS, TEXAS

Copyright © 2024 by Gerry LaFemina
All rights reserved
Printed in the United States of America

FIRST EDITION

Requests for permission to reprint or reuse
material from this work should be sent to:

Permissions
Madville Publishing
PO Box 358
Lake Dallas, TX 75065

Cover Design: Kimberly Davis
Editor Photo: Mercedes Hettich

ISBN: 978-1-956440-81-2 Paper, 978-1-956440-82-9 ebook
Library of Congress Control Number: 2023950536

Contents

1. GERRY LaFEMINA
   Introduction: The Prose Poem as Fantastic, Imaginary Creature

4. VALERIE BACHARACH
   Memento Mori

5. UJJVALA BAGAL RAHN
   Just Enough House

6. NED BALBO
   O Christmas Tree
   That Which We Discard We Also Cherish

8. MADELEINE BARNES
   Key Rock
   Self-Portrait in My Mother's Closing Lines

10. MICHELLE BONCZEK EVORY
    Absolution
    Dislocation

11. PHILLIP BORDER
    Darkness

12. RICK CAMPBELL
    Parable of the Forest Pygmy
    Forgetting the Nicene Creed

15. JOSEPH J. CAPISTA
    Myth
    Song
    Room for Error

17. GARY CIOCCO
    Being and Becoming

18. TS COODY
    Mimesis

19. CURTIS L. CRISLER
    A Comforter / A Monday / & Little Bodies

20. JIM DANIELS
    With Apology to The Tom Tom Club
    "At Last"

22 ANTHONY DiMATTEO
    Every time

23 GARY FINCKE
    The Hands

24 JEFF FRIEDMAN
    Lost Memory
    Terrorists
    Giver of Gifts

26 MOLLY FULLER
    Home Again, Home Again
    The Tale of the Flopsy Bunnies

27 JOY GAINES-FRIEDLER
    The Children's Ward
    Act 20:14
    Traveling With The Band
    Daffodils

30 GEORGE GUIDA
    Trip Wire
    The Story of a Life

31 LUKE HANKINS
    A Voice Out of the Ruins

32 GRETCHEN HEYER
    Pasiphae Answers Questions
    Missionaries Breakfasted on the Word of God
    Jute, Two inches in Diameter

34 JP HOWARD
    Dress Up

35 TOM C. HUNLEY
    Questions for Further Study
    My Chili Recipe (An Ars Poetica)

39 ANNA K. JACOBSON
    This is to That

40 PETER JOHNSON
    Vaccination, in the Broadest Sense of the Term
    Nice Socks
    Crickets

42 RICHARD JORDAN
    Jesus on the River
    Mackerel Day
    With Feathers

44 ELIZABETH KERLIKOWSKE
    Tabula Rasa
    At the 45th Parallel, Halfway Between the Equator and the North Pole

46 NINA KOSSMAN
    Kharkiv

47 JENNIFER KWON DOBBS
    Note Left at a U.S. Camptown Brothel for My Missing Imo
    Bus Stop Math

49 GERRY LaFEMINA
    Fantastic Imaginary Creatures
    Happy Pigs
    Bad Medicine

51 LAURA LAST
    Sorry

52 JOSEPH LERNER
    Black Egret

53 GERI LIPSCHULTZ
    Aphrodite in Manhattan

54 LORETTE C. LUZAJIC
    Feathers
    January River

56 GARY McDOWELL
    Prose Poem on the Nature of Things; or, Armchair Philosophy
    Another Apocalypse

58 KATHLEEN McGOOKEY
    Night Sky with Calculus Worksheet

59 JENNIFER MILITELLO
    Dear B,
    identifying the pathogen
    Antidote with Attempts at Diagnosis

62 ROBERT MILTNER
    Hopeless
    Wolf Dancing

63 ERIN MURPHY
    Hula Dancer
    Gerunding
    Ekphrasis

65 KERRY NEVILLE
    Decade

68 ROBERT PERCHAN
    The Orgun Box Junkies
    The Unselfish Elfins with their Trusty Hammers
    At Home with Marlboro Jones

71 RUBEN QUESADA
    The Cell
    To Gabriela, In Memory

72 CHRISTINE RHEIN
    Drone Pilot
    Sunday Night, Retail

74 LEE ANN RORIPAUGH
    Notes on Dissociation

78 JANE SATTERFIELD
    Abbreviated Inventory
    Latin 121

80 KATHERINE SMITH
    Crossword
    Quilt

81 JOSHUA MICHAEL STEWART
    Yellow
    Book of Love

82 VIRGIL SUÁREZ
    Chinese Weather Balloon

83 MATTHEW THORBURN
    A Hundred Birds
    How It Starts

85 ERIC TORGERSEN
    My Blindness

86 PAT VALDATA
   Mayfly

87 DOUG VAN GUNDY
   Sideshow, Barbour County Fairgrounds, 1975
   To Join the Circus

89 ELINOR ANN WALKER
   Object Impermanence
   Fugue State

91 GREG WATSON
   Why I Live in a Cold Climate

92 CATHY WITTMEYER
   Max Beckman, *Still Live with Fallen Candles*, Oil on Canvas, 1929
   Otto Dix, *Horse Cadaver*, Etching & Drypoint, 1924

94 GEORGE YATCHISIN
   Leap Year

95 MICHAEL T. YOUNG
   Sweaty Palms
   Quoting Blake to Mother

98 Contributor Notes
111 Acknowledgments

Fantastic Imaginary Creatures

An Anthology
of Contemporary
Prose Poems

INTRODUCTION: THE PROSE POEM AS FANTASTIC, IMAGINARY CREATURE

Like so many people, I have always been fascinated by the fantastic. My earliest books presented fables of talking animals and tales of mythological heroes. I learned about burning bushes in the story of Moses, about the ibis-headed god of the Egyptians, and about Ganesh, the Hindu elephant-headed god. I loved the depictions of those creatures: half human, half beast, like the minotaur, trapped in the labyrinth. So many of these wild creatures are part one thing, part another: the chimera, the sphinx, the centaur, mermaids, satyrs, kinnaras, and karuras, and even the winged Pegasus.

As I grew into elementary school, I fell in love with comic books, and loved best those superheroes with two nouns for a name: Batman, Spiderman, Moon Knight, Swamp Thing, Ghost Rider. These were names that emphasized the dichotomy of these heroes: part one thing, part another. It seemed so simple: two things in one body. And the psychology of those characters, of course, was the struggle to be whole, to be wholly both.

Is it any wonder I love the prose poem?

Two nouns define it, and yet it attempts to be its own thing while simultaneously being both prose and poetry. And what sort of prose? Fiction? Essay? The term doesn't clarify. The possibilities and permutations are limitless. The prose poem, ultimately, is something extraordinary in the garb of the ordinary. It's Peter Parker taking photos for the *Daily Bugle*—just a benign paragraph or two, until…

You get the idea.

I often think of Simic's *Dime Store Alchemy* and how it brings to the page Joseph Cornell's art: those assemblages of ordinary items in the frame of a box. How those items are imbued with so much more energy by being placed together. Viewing a Cornell box is to ask questions about how these things go together, the simple box a way into the work and a way out of the mundane. A window, if you will, and looking through it, the ordinary is made extraordinary. Simic's prose poems in *Dime Store Alchemy*, those simple boxy paragraphs, work similarly: these aren't pieces about art, but ekphrastic lyrics engaging the work, informed by the work, and made more. Criticism made into art.

I've said it before: the prose poem is the centaur, the minotaur, the fantastic imaginary creature of literature. Or, perhaps, more to the liking of my Roman Catholic upbringing, the angel or demon: part spiritual being and part of this world.

In the prose poem, of course, the prose is of this world—the recipe, the expository essay, the anecdote—and the poetic is of the other world. In Latin, *vates*, the word for poet also meant "seer, prophet, soothsayer." They were, implicitly, people who could convey with the other realm. Of course, I'm a poet, so I may be biased. That said, few people outside of the academy read poems, and perhaps it's for this very reason. "I don't get poetry," is something I hear all the time—from my students, from people I meet, even those who are self-described "avid" readers.

Give those folks a poem, and they get uncomfortable, but give them a paragraph, something that looks familiar, and they are more than willing to give it a try, to look through that window and be transported.

That's what the work in this book does: it transports and surprises and delights. I wanted to explore the possibility of the paragraph with its narrative or expository nature, and the lyric quality of the language—the musicality and held moment of delight. Some of these pieces are ekphrastic in nature like Simic's book; others explore the essay, the recipe, the narrative. Many are purely lyric. Some are fairly narrative but surprising in their fablistic sensibility, closer to those early prose poems of Aloysius Bertrand when the form was yet to be fully realized.

We live now in a time of great hybridization: from mixed martial arts to home office, from cross-over vehicles to smart watches. We live in a time of the fantastic made real, and although I don't have the flying car or jetpack I imagined I might have by now, I carry a powerful computer in my pocket, a computer that can tell me facts about anything I want. The world is far less mysterious; and mystery is what leads to both metaphor and mythology, to our desire to explain what we don't know. The sun used to be Apollo and his Chariot drawn by flying horses; thunder used to be Thor beating his hammer. Maybe that's why colleges and universities question the need for the humanities: we no longer need to wonder. Who needs Ganesh, remover of obstacles, when Google can tell you the best way to get something done? But maybe, too, that's why cryptids such as Mothman and Bigfoot capture the popular imagination, still. We need that mystery, that wildness. Maybe, too, that explains the renaissance of the prose poem in recent years, and the exploration of other hybrid texts.

I'm reminded that Thoth was the god of sacred texts, mathematics, the sciences, magic, messenger and recorder of the deities, master of knowledge, and patron of scribes. What a fantastic, imaginary creature! Perhaps Thoth was the god, too, of the prose poem. All that possibility.

Valerie Bacharach

MEMENTO MORI

I am six. A nickel from my mother for an afterschool treat. Candy necklaces, sugar dots on paper. Lips, tongue, fingers stained like watercolors. A car turns the corner, cigarette smoke wafting out an open window unearths my grandmother, her decades of smoking, fingers yellowed from nicotine. My skin has become my mother's. Thin, prone to blood pooling beneath flesh at the slightest bump. The sound of my father's voice, its terrifying frailty, when I call across three states to tell him Nathan has died. 11 p.m. Dark skies, constellations and planets. A white swallow-tailed gull circles and circles, ghostly in starlight.

JUST ENOUGH HOUSE

I want just enough house to have someplace to return to, after wandering the great outdoors like a child running ahead of its mother then circling back in a great loop to her outstretched arms. Just enough house to look out any window to see the great outdoors while still snug on a couch, as watching people go by as I sit on my mother's lap. Just enough house means when I walk back in from the porch, the living room expands like a welcoming hand. When I come back from the back patio, look through the glass-paned door, the books and desk in my study glow.

Maybe it's not enough house, because when I return from the other side of the world, or from someone else's big house, when I open the door, the ceiling seems low, the rooms small, like your mother when you visit after moving away. But in that other big house, there were more walls than windows, up the stairs like trails, cross one room after another like one state after another. It was so quiet, I started to forget there was a world outside.

Ned Balbo

O CHRISTMAS TREE

It was finally time for Christmas to end, and none too soon. The worst part was the tree. It had entered the house naked, trickling sap and shedding needles, but, day by day, had grown triumphant. Now, it stood in splendor, hogging everyone's attention, indifferent to those who'd served its secret purpose. Silver-garlanded, it shone; tinsel-bedecked, it masqueraded, pretending that showers of ice had caught it, friendless, under a winter sky.

Its arrival had felt obscene. Its pitted trunk, cylindrical, was as thick as a man's wrist, cleanly cut where someone's axe had swung full force. Not mine. I get my trees at the lot. It's too much work to climb up hills, lugging saws and coils of rope, trying to shut out the false cheer of families singing like Von Trapps. But someone had cut it down, sweating through the confrontation, adding to the rows of neatly severed stumps.

Now the corpse was mine. Festooned with vintage ornaments, chipped trumpets with coiled stems, and Santa, Santa everywhere, his incarnations shedding light on his activities through the year: Santa surfing, Santa bathing, Santa playing electric guitar. A church from 1950 holds the light of a bulb it swallowed, resting quietly on a piano fallen silent.

You entered nude and now you're clothed—in kitsch, recovered memories. You watch from your place of honor, judging the depth of our betrayals, the hidden history of our bond. Colors change and paint the ceiling. Will someone blow the trumpets soon? Will someone tear your fragile garments, watch them shatter against the floor? Who'll sweep up the shards, the needles?

I suspect that, as so often, the ugly chore will fall to me, the father whose lack of courage fails to prove his common sense; whose family hides in the basement, blinded and burned by sparks of light, waiting for the rain of fire, the shock, the blackout.

THAT WHICH WE DISCARD WE ALSO CHERISH

Everybody liked to go the dump when I was a kid. My father and I were no exception. Station wagons rattled over the pitted old dirt road. Tailgates spat out bags of trash, push-mowers damaged beyond repair, so many dented or twisted dolls they could have filled a school bus.

No one stood at the chain-link gate to check the decal on our windshield. This was in pre-decal days when people came and went at will.

The stench was overwhelming, but no one seemed to mind.

This was back in the days when no one questioned what was right. Trash rotting away a stone's throw from the trees of your backyard? No problem! This was progress.

Metal and plastic decomposed, chemicals leached into the soil, but everyone knew they'd disappear and had to be harmless anyway.

A smashed bicycle wheel spun slowly in summer wind. You didn't want to stand downwind. On all sides, hills of rubbish rose higher than we could reach. Kids climbed over the garbage cliff-heaps, testing their foothold in the junk. "Look, a G.I. Joe! And only one of his legs is missing!"

Dad and I dragged out the trash bags that held the remains of our lawn—great bundles of soft wet clumps, brown tufts like dried shag carpet. You could only keep so much of it.

But here in the dump, there was no limit to what you could find. We never stayed as long as I wanted. Someone's transistor radio tuned to an AM station broadcast static and the Rolling Stones with equal urgency.

Even today, I see the children that I glimpsed as we drove off. They looked like orphans hopping the fence, picking through milk cartons and boxes, inspecting rags while oil drums burned and poured black smoke into the sky.

Madeleine Barnes

KEY ROCK

assignment: find a pen (any color) and paper (any size) and draw a picture of your first home. Sketch the kitchen, the basement, attic, pantry, the hallways you were too afraid to walk after a nightmare. was your bed beside a window? if your house was surrounded by trees, what kind? when there was nowhere to go, where would people try to find you? shade in the spaces that were yours. circle the spaces that were not. what did you want that you didn't have; what did you have that you didn't need; what did you think about and who did you talk to? show me a porch, a pool, a favorite chair, a blanket, a tablecloth, a cup of blueberries, an ironing board. what did you find that was meant to be hidden? when were you held; by whom were you ignored? who folded your clothes? were the animals outside real or unreal? where did you eat breakfast, do your homework, tell a lie just to see if you could? describe the sound of the doorbell and, if you can, note the lights. are they on? what did you forgive, and how? under which rock was the spare key kept? did someone mark the key with nail polish? what color? we had one, too—a decoy, a fake stone with a panel that slid open, space for two small keys. it wasn't hard to locate. it led to everything we owned. i want to remember what you remember, to hide where you hide, to keep track of every detail, to know how to find you by way of soil, stone, door.

SELF-PORTRAIT IN MY MOTHER'S CLOSING LINES

my mother is writing a poem about us. struggling to finish it, she calls and says, tell me where you want to wind up. I say, together, with books, somewhere like the park, neither of us working. the end of capitalism. free healthcare. she says: i like those words. in her poem, i live in a studio apartment. in real life, i live in her poem. in the afterlife, we live—where? i mean, where do we want to end up? in her poem, we swim with elephants, an image from a dream i had months after a friend jumped off the brooklyn bridge. every time i cross it, i remember how he said that his main problem was not knowing how to love himself enough. why couldn't i hear the emergency in those words? his smile, his shrug. in his last email to me he wrote, thanks for your letter, you're a sweet sweet girl. years ago, my mother told me that i have something every woman in our family has: resilience. this word, so close to silence, re-silence. studies show that resilience isn't necessarily innate, it's learned, it requires practice. from whom do we learn to love ourselves enough? she calls again: hi, just sent the final draft, let me know what you think about the ending. i want to say, it's your poem, you have to choose, but I know how she'll respond: come on, work with me.

Michelle Bonczek Evory

ABSOLUTION

Chapter one: she contemplates, chooses. Chapter two: broken glass and flames, red clouds burning blue like blood on her doctor's smock the day before the appointment. Something has decided she has no choice but to have and name him. Chapter three: ripped tissue and stitches, her uterus bursts and is scooped out. Chapter four: her breasts wither. Chapter five: she raises him on Chapter six: baseball, burgers, and Chapter seven: bugs in jars. She kisses his head and he grows tall, likes girls. Chapter eight: he likes guns and ropes more than girls like him. Chapter nine. Chapter ten. Chapter eleven: one girl plus one rope plus one gun plus three bullets equals he's fifteen. Chapter twelve: someone decides he knew what he was doing. Chapter thirteen: Marshall sits still for his injection. Few protesters this time. Finally, rain. His mother lets it drip from her eyelashes and wishes she were chapter fourteen: the fertile earth taking him back.

DISLOCATION

I was hiking when my torso, it twisted. My left arm, it fell out. I felt the two knobs where my shoulder had been, swept my finger across the bottom of the empty cup. When my husband saw me fall he said Oh shit. Three men ahead on the trail came back. I couldn't move. My husband lifted his binoculars and looked downriver. He handed them to the strangers who took turns looking and shaking their heads. I could see the shadow of my arm reaching out of the rapids. I could hear the river cry out for help.

DARKNESS

After school, I would run off into the forest behind my grandmother's house, reinventing myself as a knight or angel sent to vanquish earth's remaining demons. One evening, once I had whacked my wooden sword down to a stub, I came across a large black dog that seemed to be waiting for me in the treaded path. He wagged his tail friendly; thus, I decided God sent the beast to aid me in my crusade, and fashioned a new sword from a black oak to dub the mongrel, Darkness, for he would send our enemies to an everlasting sleep.

Darkness was my only friend in those days. Always waiting for me in the shadows of the woods until one afternoon in late November, when the white tails and the black bears head deeper into the forest, he didn't appear.

I thought he must have gone on without me, so I drew my battered sword and charged deep into the brush; believing he was already in the middle of the fight, I searched for Darkness till I found a trail of blood and followed it to the three black holes through his chest.

Rick Campbell

PARABLE OF THE FOREST PYGMY

There's a story about a forest pygmy who's taken (not by force, but maybe tricked, not fully informed consent) out of the jungle canopy on to the savannah and he freezes, panics like a stoned hippie before a leering cop, then falls to the ground and covers his head. The space, the vastness of everything, the horizon stretching to the other end of the earth is too much for him. He's a level-headed, respected, experienced, worldly pygmy—a man among men in his own world and that's his problem. His known world, his points of reference, definition, boundary are gone and suddenly he's outside, exposed to who the hell knows what. There's only a finite number of things that can kill a pygmy in the jungle; it may seem ever so large when the killer comes: panthers, lions, snakes, even those ants that swarm down the trees and descend upon the more careless pygmies or more likely the foolish and uninformed European who got tired, or drugged on some exotic jungle berry's juice. Even though a pygmy can't always see what's coming, at least he knows it's nearby. There's a learned level of alertness that will usually protect him and if the panther gets him anyway or he's trampled by the occasional but not totally random stampeding things that look like pigs, and maybe they are (a pygmy would know)—well, he tried. He can take small comfort knowing he was killed by a known danger, the same collection of dangers that have killed many generations of his ancestors. As they say, in some more deterministic cultures, it was his time to go and the panther's time to eat. *But not this pygmy.* He's on the savannah, the plain, the plateau; he doesn't even have a name for it, even though it apparently has dozens of names. He can't even say what it looks like—flat, open, empty, sparse, desolate, bright, burnt sienna. He can't say gazelle, wildebeest, jackal, rhino, Jeep, Land Rover. He probably has a word for dangerous, for fear, but it's too small for this. He probably even has a phrase for *oh shit what's that?* This pygmy just curls up in a ball, a fetal position; his anthropologist "friend" might, if he isn't a totally cruel jerk, gather the pygmy into his arms and say in a rough, but close enough for anthropology translation: "it's ok Frankie; it's just the savannah" (which as we know means nothing to poor Frankie) and lead him gently back to the cover of the panther and python filled forest. A grad student will be taking notes of course, or a film crew getting every touching and strange moment, but at least our pygmy will go home not too worse for wear, except for the lifetime of nightmares he will have where something silent and large comes out of the sky that never ends in a world where there's no place to hide and it's always too bright and burning and it snatches him up and he's gone, maybe forever, maybe just a night and then again the next night and the next.

FORGETTING THE NICENE CREED

Father Mike was ecstatic. He'd looked at a convenience store clerk and saw the Risen Lord and now he forgot to say the Creed. Half the congregation knelt, half stood; I reverted to catholic legalisms and wondered if this mass—highest of all, ritual of resurrection, cornerstone of faith, would count. What if this topples the tower and this little church and its hundred souls invalidate Easter. Jesus not risen? Stone not rolled away? Mary M still weeping about a stolen body? There's a reason for liturgy, I wanted to shout. You believe in one God. What now about all things visible & invisible & Jesus—begotten not made, of one substance w/the father? What of that? How after you forget do you go back? It's not fair that I, who do not believe in any of this anymore, should record thy fault. I used to make up sins to confess when I'd yet to learn real ones, and now I'm trapped with you, real sin on my soul and you forget your Creed. He shall come back to judge the quick & the dead. I may be among the quick *saying not me. I knew he should have said it.*

Maybe this isn't sin, just Grievous Technical Fault, like when I wore the orange stars and moon shirt to my Grandmother's funeral. That wasn't held against her, I don't think, not me, either. Though who's to say what I would have become if blessed. Rich? Famous? Handsome? A drummer in a rock and roll band? I believed once in a holy, catholic & apostolic church, though then I didn't know what apostolic meant. I never looked for the resurrection of the dead. Maybe because our priest was never excited, never so swept by passion that he threw his arms open and raised them over all of us to cry *the Lord is Risen, and we are all the Risen Lord*. I think this too was once a sin, the Gospel of Thomas maybe. Too too much *Kingdom of God is inside of you*. Too close to the pagan, made more for peace and love, not colonialism and manifest destiny.

What if Jesus is and is pissed? What if we blew it? This day's always been suspect in my book. Easter, the day you say He rose from the dead, rides our calendar like a rubber duck bobbing on carnival water. Moveable feast, we call it, to hide our confusion. If the Resurrection was going to be this fucking important, some scribe or apostle should have checked his day planner and jotted a note: *Jesus rose today*, not just some day after the spring equinox. Be more specific, for god's sake. That too, was not my doing. So should suddenly You become a wrathful god rather than a tad merciful, in case there's merit and consequence in all of this, the rite of the Eucharist, body & blood & magic, in case we are to follow ALL the rules, this one especially that they are toying with so cavalierly, in case you were thinking of smiting & smoting this little church to ash, please spare me and my family. We looked at each other, not as risen lords, but because we caught the error.

We wanted to say that you were incarnate by the holy spirit of the Virgin Mary, made man and crucified (for us), that you were buried & rose & ascended. I've been reading the Book of Common Prayer now for an hour. In case You were *thinking of feeding us the bread of tears, giving our crops to caterpillars, wiping us out of the book of the living, letting our enemies' dogs lick our blood*, remember (can you even forget?) it wasn't our doing. Ok, I don't Believe but I do believe that liturgy is liturgy. Yes, I've sung with too much glee Patti Smith's *Jesus died for somebody's sins but not mine*. Still, if Father Mike had said it I would have remembered years of saying it and some of them in earnest. I still cringe a little when these Episcopalians add the extra words to your prayer our Father. No, I don't dwell in the shelter of the most high, but I have learned to number my days. I believe we might, at any time, be *swept away like a dream, fade suddenly like the grass. We are but flesh, a breath that goes forth and does not return*.

MYTH

Cross a thin ribbon of sky which is, of course, the river. A child pits a bowl of olives with the bone-handled paring knife. Its blade is whetted too thin; it holds everyone's reflection but her own. She is eight. Off with your finger she says to no one, then lops off a tip, pinches its skin, and extracts with her teeth the olive pit, which she spits into another bowl. Three bowls, in all: one for what is hard, one for what is soft, one for what remains untouched. From the hook she has lifted, draped along her neck, and tied at the small hollow of her back the night. Clock, upon clock, upon clock. Still, who is prepared for this moment? If you want to hear better, close your eyes, she says. If you want to hear better, cover your ears. Each olive in the yellow bowl is black. Lining the river bridge are houses identical to this house; windows on one side hold the world, but windows on the other side hold the world. She counts sparrows on ratlines. When you stop dreaming of ghosts, she explains, then you have become a ghost. When she dreams, the olives in her dreams are green.

SONG

Picture the hive as a heart on a wire twenty-feet overhead beside the transformer————————picture paper awhirr in delicious stammer as swarm diagrams a grammar of murmur————————as alit little letters unset to unsettle————————love, twenty years later I found on a

wire our	how	first kiss, that buzz,
not gone—	lively how	—just transfigured
————	deadly how wing	by a posey of wasps
to this heart	and how stinger	on a wire————
heart on a	how not quite	wire.
	of earth nor	
	neither of	
	ether	

ROOM FOR ERROR

Mine's a Wunderkammer of chock-full keepsakes catalogued according to shame and functionality: here lie unshelved hagiographies I've read from back to front, here sherds of clay on which I trace repeatedly the names of those who I profess to love, here beside a pyx of stubby cigarettes and honey flasks I've brimmed with piss, six thumb-worm poor box coins I'll heave at the deck of a 5' 9" swallow tail between whose foam and fiberglass is lodged the skull of my nextborn. It's true: the divan and settee are not on speaking terms. It's true: magniloquence begins at home. I am capable of patience, empathy, and graciousness only rarely. Excuse those grease spots on the wall where the minotaur reclines, excuse the piled icons, excuse this slug I'll never puzzle back into its casing. Admire, though, the skeletons of my four best horses who grazed steppes and licked cool water from my fingertips. Admire the two blue amphorae and the cask of bezoar stones. Admire the plaque outside the door: *Bidden or un-bidden, present is god.*

BEING AND BECOMING

Being from this country called Pennsylvania I know all about the accents the dreariness the cold the snow the heat the sun the rivers that divide us and flood us with both joy and death with their peaceful or raging waters the sports teams that excite and enrage us the opioids that have devastated us ravaged us the mountain laurel that become mountains the mountains that become frozen and picturesque the lack of sun in Pittsburgh the lack of New York in Philly. This country called Pennsylvania has an East and a West a Southeast and Southwest a Northeast and a South Central. It contains multitudes and attitudes it sits on and beside West Virginia and knocks up against New York New Jersey and Ohio. Being from it and in it I become its hills valleys and hollers and it becomes becoming to me. Becoming as a lake in late August whose ripples resonate with what is has been and could not be.

TS Coody

MIMESIS

I.

The hive sings tabernacle. Mother says I am not to be here, an ice cream melting in one hand and three dying bees in the palm of the other. So dead-alive. The bees need sugar. Their wings beat the saddest chord on my tongue.

II.

Dark as incense. Sacred as a church altar. This is the room of mother, father, fever, night terror. Purple shag smoked mirrors velvet bedspread. Come now the bees from outside in, following the sun's tongue through a tiny crevice, orange-rind thin. A full beard of sisters and the old queen, churning and writhing in one golden wave, dripping bees like overspray. Are they confused as they fall to the bruised plush below? What is this wooly grass?

III.

I cannot recall which came first: the word or the humming thing in my mouth. Did I manifest the bristles and the stylets and yes, even the honey with an ecstatic, breathy digraph? What sound do the bees make in Spain? Istanbul? I cannot speak the word with a mouth full of bees. The bees do all the talking.

A COMFORTER / A MONDAY / LITTLE BODIES

The snow deputized Monday's moodiness / crunch by crunch / under boots / under an overcast firmament / My parka and gloves asked if I was warm / Uh-huh / The comforter / too much for my Maytag / got pelted with parachuting, slow-mo, white angels / falling to earth / like ash from chimneys / A Catholic lip balm if in stigmata / A papal remembrance / Nothing like religion to hold us hostage / Something mean about gas showers made me SMH / War, with its blotches / I hugged comforter, tighter, /before breaking threshold of laundromat / Transformed back to little / Carrying my smaller sister through projects / We, cold / Breath, cloudy / I, big brother / made her laugh to forget winter / thrashing at her exposed nose and lips / to forget projects / I had no compulsion for shape-shifting / then / She was a sparkling little planet round my neck / A smile I hated to see cry / Something that frightened me / How parents lose their shit when the screen door shuts / and we / the children / are on fire, outside / No threats / other than Mother Nature / pushing us back / towards home / before other threats could pounce / But big bros crowd little sisters / I knew nothing of balance / That a multitude of feathers can hold some weight / Hell, I was fledgling too / "You watch the back. I got the front. Ok?" / "Ok," she boomeranged back, in little girl. "Nothing but a bunch of snow!" She laughed / I shook her body / She laughed harder / In little bits / a comforter brought us back / Ghetto- kids shlepping through winds wanting to capture the heat from childhood / Now, my sis lives in Austin / Doesn't care to listen to January's sass / Is it because I'm not sludging / Mama's baby / in a bear-hug / through winter / to get us home? / No / her dreams grew hungrier / She just learned new ways to taste survival ///////

Jim Daniels

WITH APOLOGY TO THE TOM TOM CLUB

"The Genius of Love" was the only major hit song by the Tom Tom Club

Do you ever feel like you're the Genius of Love, walking absolutely not the word for what you are doing, down the sidewalk, across the crosswalk? I mean cross-strut, talking in tongues like a half-wit one-hit wonder. We can go our whole lives without finding our recognizable groove, and if you are not the Genius of Love perhaps you can be the Idiot Savant of Love for having stumbled into a cosmic hip-sway, the deep surge of the universe, the comet of your silly grin perhaps due to the unforecast weather of eye contact with ten people in a row including two ecstatic babies in strollers and a wheelchair-bound friend waiting for another friend in her wheelchair and they joke about racing and you are almost apologetic until they are out of sight, then bust the move again, shouting aloud beneath the caressing cathedral of lush green trees in the park, *Where did that come from?* And oh, the genius shrug of wind through branches.

"AT LAST"

was the bridal dance at his first two weddings. I admit the wistful sway-beats were better than Seger's "Old Time Rock and Roll" and Elvis' "Can't Help Falling in Love With You." We sighed "At Last" when he didn't marry the fourth one. He had a baby with the second one. She wouldn't marry him. Took the money behind the curtain instead. They all looked alike in white dresses and misplaced optimism. Game-show loser, at last he gave up marrying. The chocolate fountain covered my son's first white shirt. It wouldn't be his last. White shirts for all occasions. You can't go wrong with white if you're uncertain. White tux or black? He was always uncertain. He changed his mind about changing his mind. Dreams cramped his style, which was to not dream. He fixed old pinball machines on the side. He specialized in illegal fireworks shows. He was a kid in a candy store that only sold toxic candy. He had a sweet tooth for toxic. First, it was the swinging neighbors, then the dogs that bit. He got custody of the daughter just when she started to hate her life and everyone in it. At last. They served lame hors d'oeuvres—carrots and celery and dip. What did he do with all the wedding money? Was it some Ponzi scheme? He was just *Looking for love in...* etc... At last, his wispy moustache grew in—just in time to turn gray. He disowned himself in a ritual ceremony, then rode a rocket into space for the grand finale. At last, nobody said, though we might have been thinking it. They dressed him in white since it was his first and only time. We took leftovers for our son, who had no appetite for wakes. The overpriced photo albums of equal weight and thickness created imbalanced mockery in a dim-lit corner of the home. Get my good side, he always said—let me pause here for a second while the song ends at last—then he blew it off. Good food at the wake. Don't be cruel. The lasagna had some special sauce that kept us from crying.

Anthony DiMatteo
EVERY TIME

is the first time because for you it's never been that way before, the ocean that is, when come upon along the shore and the waves look like horses racing, but that's true of a lot of things, your hair in the morning tossed like an upside-down flame, or the dog's poop as if a ziggurat, or the slant of the sun through the reeds looking like a prisoner. Everything gets to have its own wrack line and its own majesty. Even memory's a glow worm with a future sliding into the present moment and arriving there dockside where you were counting the seconds between waves and how your mother counted heads for supper popped into your head. Every time is the last time it will ever come again. This is why the Greeks said Eros is the youngest and oldest of the gods, also known as Phanes or "the one who happens" in the beginning of time that has no end birthed out of the belly of night with each sunrise a light that will never come again, a phenomenon in search of a name, each moment the edge of eternity.

THE HANDS

In magazines and newspapers, my great uncle, for decades, was a hand model. According to my father, those hands looked as if they had never done a day's work, even in age, smooth, white, untouched. My father's hands were always white with flour, dusted to roll dough into spheres, left and right handed, to model forms for sandwich buns while I relied upon the right, unable, after seven years of Friday night work, to master the art of left-handed circles. Years before, bare-handed, a man had pulled a pan of sandwich buns from the oven without burning his hands. My father, some Fridays, would tell that story whenever miracles were mentioned. As if we needed faith while that man never again forgot his gloves. As if we needed to believe a woman born with three fingers experienced, after amputation, a phantom hand with five fingers. As if those bones had needed years of weather to expose them. Now, my daughter, an artist, teaches anatomy to small children, beginning, each year, with the hands. Miraculously, her daughter, at five, drew my hands like a camera. My mother had a small scrapbook of clipped ads that featured hands. Here, she said, are your uncle's, and there, too. Looking was like taking an IQ test. Which of these are identical? Which one of those doesn't belong? My mother's uncle lived forty years beyond modeling, his hands so unspotted for so long they seemed to suggest that his body was unspeakably pink and soft.

Jeff Friedman

LOST MEMORY

My sister stole a memory of mine from my house and took it home, hidden in her coat. I couldn't remember the memory, but there was an empty space on the sideboard under the window. "Give me back the memory," I said, standing outside her door. "And I won't report you to the authorities." She let me in. "Don't be ridiculous," she said. "Why would I steal a memory of yours?" It didn't take me long to find the memory, a blue jar sitting on the glass stand between two chairs. When I picked it up, she looked puzzled. "This is my place," she said. "These are my things." "Not true," I replied and unscrewed the lid. Emptiness wafted out with its stinging scent. Now I remembered something I had wanted to forget. I screwed the lid back on quickly and set it down. "That's my memory," she said. "You shouldn't have opened it." "Then what do you remember?" I asked. "Nothing—it's gone because you let it out." And as I stood there, angry at my sister, the scent of the memory evaporated, and all I could remember was the jar, and now that belonged to her.

TERRORISTS

We found them in cafes, sipping Americanos at tables near windows, ready to detonate bombs with their smart watches. We found them wheeling carts through the supermarket, testing the avocados for ripeness, bagging up chickpeas and figs. We found them in windows disguised as mannikins, sharply tailored, their faces perfectly calm. We found them in our neighborhoods, burying their weapons in flower gardens and laying down bags of mulch. We found them in the faces of the clouds, in the dust falling over us. We found pieces of their stars and the shards of the exploding moon. We found their swirling gases, their sloughed skins, their muted masks. They entered our homes, vibrating in our networks, blurring our screens. Day and night, we heard them humming our songs, chanting our names, talking with our voices.

GIVER OF GIFTS

Before the old man went under, he sang one of his miserable songs, for which he is famous. He praised onions for their character, ducks for their communal spirit, and carpenter ants for their strong jaws and endurance. "So what if they don't win any races." He kissed each of us on the cheek, "for the last time," he said, his breath stinking of horseradish and garlic. "Be kind," he said, which he never was. He praised chicken fat, the four bellies of the cow, the croaking frogs that "scared the shit out of Pharaoh," with whom he split lox and bagel at the Carnegie deli on Wednesdays. He cursed the evil demented president and all his sycophants. He cursed the confederate senator blocking every bill, his wattle trembling, the attorney general bloating like a stuffed turkey. He begged us to follow the righteous path and give up vanity. He asked that we light candles for him, repeat his words, tell stories of his life. He asked that his memories become seeds that we plant in the wind. He called himself the last Babylonian king, spreading literacy to the masses. He called himself a "giver of gifts," though he never donated to any causes or even dropped a nickel in a beggar's cup. He praised himself for his journey in the desert, his days running with the hyenas, his devotion to a small bird that died in his hand. Then he closed his eyes and went under. At last, there was no pulse or breath, no preaching, only peace. But in the morning, he began to sing another of his miserable songs, and before he went under again, we had to repeat the whole damn ceremony.

Molly Fuller

HOME AGAIN, HOME AGAIN

The mulberry tree grows girls between its roots each spring. They poke up their soft, fuzzy heads and nibble the four leaf clovers that we gather and leave for them on rocks the size of dinner plates. We watch them grow tall and lean, long-haired and beautiful. The stars reflect in the island iris of each dark eye as we saddle them up, holding their long braids like reins, and ride them to market to see what price they will fetch.

THE TALE OF THE FLOPSY BUNNIES

All the girls in the yellow wing of the hospital give birth to rabbits at the same time in the same day. The nurses bundle them up in pink and blue. The new mothers coo and rub their soft, velvet heads. They call them by the names they have rehearsed for sons and daughters. The fathers smoke cigars and drink whiskey. The grandmothers weep and knit bonnets with holes for small ears. The grandfathers watch from their rockers, peeling carrots for stew.

THE CHILDREN'S WARD

At night we breathed in rhythm to the iron lung that hulled the boy on his back, whose face could be seen only in the rectangle of mirrored glass above him. Bodacious and afraid we were untrained soldiers—our street clothes missing, our lives given over to the alien tongues of hospital staff, the polished metal of gurneys and pitchers of water. The windows so far above our heads, we could only guess the life outside: birds flitting tree to tree, the park bench empty then not. A few of us played together but never where that boy lay cased in that crude metal tube, afraid of that foreign country, and what we might see there. Funny, how much I loved him when I went over there by myself, dared to look in that mirror.

ACT 20:14

I saved a fly today—or, I should say, I gave it a way to save itself. Does that make me a god? Does putting water to the roots of roses, to the roots of trees? Does washing the dishes? And while I'm satisfied with the motion of soap-soaked sponge to dish I'm thinking how my sister never calls. But when was the last time I called her? We're all waiting for I'm sorry to be disturbed by our presence, to fly out of its protection like a moth in the shade of a boxwood. I can't explain survival or what's behind it. Another friend closed the door on our future today; claims her voice isn't heard. But, her voice, like anyone else's is hidden inside her own failure to speak. There isn't much I can do about that. Though I'd like to. Oh how I envy the happy drunk, her ability to fly outside her pain, her great trick of escape. My mother once wrote a letter. Sent it to each of us. She wrote, You kids are wonderful despite me. Doesn't a plea disguised, deserve mercy? I can't explain why I threw that letter out. I can't explain why I lured the fly to the screen door by closing all the blinds; how I knew it would find the light.

TRAVELING WITH THE BAND

We're headed to California, equipment loaded in the backbeat of a station wagon, Michael driving, smoking a Lucky, the road sings *yes, yes yes* matching the rhythm of hostility's dissipating snare. Go ahead condemn me. I come from the School of Defiance where girls uninterested in cake-making are activists, champions of the underdog, rooters for the left handed music makers. I waded, waited for this chance

to throw off those lonely headphones where I let Zeppelin spin a whole lotta' love around my head, my elbows rooted to the carpet in my room, I waited, waded through the next lie from my boyfriend & the next boyfriend & the next lie. Still, I wanted them, their desire infused with mine, the way Coltrane describes Truth as indestructible & innovation as departure from the customary. Maybe lies are just a small dispute with change,

& creativity, a way out from the airlessness of convention. Except, accept the hurt. Let it become Van Gogh tree branches, curly as my hair. Michael is smoking a Lucky Strike. I am in the car with him, the drums, an amp, his Fender guitar, heading south to Padre Island, where for a month there will be a piano in my room. Then on to Colorado where Michael & I will trip up the mountains to Pike's Peak into the blues, blue, bluest

sky I've ever seen, where the *urge for going* is, for me, the antidote to indignity, self-imposed outcast, choosing to cast out, leave, humiliation, sucker punches, leave it; leave the damn wallpaper behind.

DAFFODILS

The street we walked home from school was austere; trees twiggy saplings of suburbia, houses compact repetitions of life after war. The neighborhood was a model girl with an expense account. A purse to match each outfit, no lush gardens, just a few spring flowers outside Mrs. Goddeson's house. What did I know of bulbs, or the hands that planted them? I left the sidewalk, even though it meant non-conformity, crossed her carpet of lawn, pulled on the thick stems that would not release. Someone was sure to see me. Someone was already marking me. I pulled at the stubborn flowers until I felt something tear. A breaking from its roots. A release. Frightened and willing I held the whole of it. I am responsible for this life—this certain death.

George Guida

TRIP WIRE

We fear the reason we're on the run. The wire runs across the transom. Night falls only as warning. The ghost never stumbles on its ghostly visage stubble. The wire runs across the bathroom kleigs. The delivery man's left packages in our eyes. We're blind to the wire's ends. We can't see all the places the wire will run invisible. Don't tell. I've cut the wire. Don't tell. I've taken the wire. The wire coils like—not a snake, not a key ring, not an easy notion. I've renamed the wire. The times demand a substitute for vigilance. The threats are imminent and always have been. I've been carrying the wire for centuries. Don't tell. We've been on the run since before we could fall.

THE STORY OF A LIFE

I was young. I met a woman. We made each other happy. We made each other sad. We took in a dog, who was our child. First he went blind, then we tired of struggle. Someone pretty came along. I followed her. The woman I loved killed me off. She lives a life always meant for her. She is the only one who knew. I married the pretty girl and the old dog died. We have a child and make each other sad. We stay together. For the child or not. At night I read him stories until he asks me to shut the light. In the darkness I lie on the floor by his bed. I follow this plot as though it weren't mine. When he falls asleep, I close my eyes.

Luke Hankins

A VOICE OUT OF THE RUINS

Nostalgia for a place I've never been. Remembered intimacy with a person I've never known. A voice out of the ruins of Eden, calling me back, not into Eden, but into what is possible there, where Eden once stood, in the ruins.

Gretchen Heyer

PASIPHAE ANSWERS QUESTIONS

Erotic passages scatter around me like rotting plums. Otherwise, you would not be asking. No, I cannot recall the sky to be clear or pale blue. This is as much as I can say about the encounter. Yes—the leak, the glow, the vanishing. I remain a set of impressions, harsh ones lasting longer, like squares of colored glass in a frame. Was I a flirt? Strangers say of me—*you know that one, the bull got too close.* I can tell you how light dangled through the heat. A sweet and slightly grainy liquid covered my thighs. I am sure none of you recall I ran towards the sea, believing waves could not stretch far enough my direction. The sky both clear and pale blue. I tell you this because I know you want some version of why.

MISSIONARIES BREAKFASTED ON THE WORD OF GOD

We sat with spoons in the air. Adults piled bowls and plates, murmuring gratitudes. We children stared out the window towards dead grass of the soccer field, keeping our backs to their smoldering. We measured distance from table to mouth. Once, I tried to hold a bite on my tongue long enough to walk outside and spit it out, examine it for flakes and textures. The Word of God tasted of cotton candy minus sugar. The Word of God dissolved so fast I never got a good look at what it was made of. I lived with heavy doubt. I covered the skyline with hunger. The Word of God roamed around my stomach. Every time I wondered what made me, I burped.

JUTE, TWO INCHES IN DIAMETER

One end burned my thumb. The other out there somewhere. I carried provisions, insects, sealed memories. The cushion of clouds pressed down on me. The cushion with a hole. *Like a door,* you said. I never believed you. I heard my mother, always so logical and matter of fact. My mother warned me of touch and thought so I could not listen to you. I stood in the swamp among the mangroves that told how to breathe through water. Ok, so I heard them. They shouted—left no confusion on closing bark mouths at high tide, opening them at low. Guides show up in costume. From where you stood, my story had a logic that never existed. Mud. Everywhere mud. Stench of dead fish. Wispy gold eyes like bullets. Baby alligators at my toes—paleolithic hordes with pinchers. A few lights rose out of the fog. Receded. I followed the rope.

JP Howard

DRESS UP

*if I could hold memory this would be the snap-
shot: babygirl, happy with yourself, a splash
of pastels: powder blue, pale pink, Mama's
lemon striped dress falling off your shoulders.
Isn't that her sunday best wig, under that big
church hat? tilted, tipped, tickling, you all
giggles going on an adventure through your
Sugar Hill apartment all those oversized Mama
bags packed for the trip those French doors
leading to a land faraway*

QUESTIONS FOR FURTHER STUDY

1. How are these poems like dark dad jokes with Gillette® razors in them and wild slept-on hair and a receding hairline all the punchlines lost like a wedding ring swallowed by a toddler sitting on a potty chair learning that *this is going to hurt us more than it hurts you* is just one of life's pretty lies like the one about birdsong and poetry both being peaceful and chime-like when really both are elaborate ways of saying *let's get it on* or *stay out of my tree*?

2. Is it possible to write something original about turning fifty what would Keats have written about turning fifty had he turned fifty will my name be written on ice with spray paint or carved into a tree next to my wife's name or whispered into our grandkids' ears soft as snow falling on the wings of a dead bird?

3. What is the symbolism of the light in the puddle the Buffalo-shaped ache the soap bubble the skipping stone and if the author were truly a good father would he for real compare his kids to Bigfoot or write poems like flashlights shining in their eyes?

4. Have you or anyone you know made it through *Remembrances Of Things Past* have you felt the loss of someone you never really knew have you seen through the color blue into its constituents magenta and cyan have you felt like there's something wrong with you but you never knew what until you read about it in a book and if so did you hate the book and its author or did you feel grateful like the time you were about to sing "The Star Spangled Banner" before a baseball game with toilet paper clinging to your shoe when a bat boy jogged up to you, pointed out the toilet paper, pulled it off, and disposed of it in the dugout?

5. Do these poems move across your heart a) like tumbleweeds across a desert b) like wind gusts blown in from the sea or c) like the beautiful new person at work who gets promoted before learning your name?

6. Where children are concerned is it fair to say that the heart is Santa's sleigh weighed down by an impossible load the heart a small thing dragged across the night by large animals?

7. Is adopting a scared teenager more like trying to garden on a scarred battlefield or like insisting on the day-olds at Dunkin Donuts is it like rescuing meat from a grinder in some kind of PETA-inspired intervention and then trying with all you have not to become the meat not to become the grinder?

8. Is autism the beginning of a new stage of consciousness what would you say to the loneliest whale in the world if he could hear or understand you if you could hear his lonely 52-Hertz cry just lower than the lowest note on a tuba inaudible even to other whales?

9. Is it possible to die from a broken heart to dream yourself into a better self to have an allergic reaction to water what is the probability of being born one in 400 trillion according to some guy on the Internet wow here we are somehow here IRL and on the WWW how does anyone ever yawn and why can't we all live every moment in awe like Adam at the moment when he first saw Eve or like the first Cro-Magnon to gaze at a bison and paint it on the cave wall?

MY CHILI RECIPE (AN ARS POETICA)

I. Whatcha Need

the river
3 pounds ground beef
the passing of the dead on the banks of what remains
4 Tbsp. minced garlic
a galloping sound
2 diced green peppers
the sound of a violin being shattered by a perfectionist
1 diced onion

the wind, humming half-drunkenly

1 16oz. can red kidney beans

the song of nuns calming children during a hurricane

1 beer

the four seasons

1 16oz. can pinto beans

a mouth full of vowels and air

6 bay leaves

every ache in your body

2 16oz. cans of corn

thee and *thou* and *thy* and the way all three make your tongue feel under your teeth

3 tsp. salt

Agamemnon's last cry and the sound of his spear whistling in the Trojan wind

3 Tbsp. sugar

the long process of two people becoming a couple

1 Tbsp. chili powder

the words you need when you're untethered from yourself

3 Tbsp. Dale's seasoning sauce

the sound of that violinist trying again

2 15oz. cans diced tomatoes

the words that bring the world back when it's floating away like a helium balloon

1 tsp. black pepper

breaking up & making up

1 8oz. can tomato sauce

the odor of the Library of Alexandria burning

2 Tbsp. vinegar

the prayer of a dying man, veiled in anagrams

3 serrano peppers

all of your sorrows

II. Whatcha Do

Begin with the river. Brown beef and memories of the dead with garlic, green peppers, the heartsong of the near-shattered violinist, and onion. Love the world the way a horse's spirit gallops in its body. Add the whistles of wind, the nunsong, the mouthfuls of air and vowels, the *thee* and the *thy* and the *thou*, the ache of human pangs, the spear shivering in midair, the long process of becoming a couple, the words you need to bring yourself back to yourself. Add Dale's after draining grease.

Add heat and ingredients, starting with seasonings. Add the seasons. Sprinkle in sighs and songs, the sound of the violin trying again, the words you need to bring the world back to the world. Slowly bring to boil. Add beer and beans, the tide, corn, tomatoes, and tomato sauce. Add bay leaves and breakups followed by makeups. Put all of your sorrows into the anagrammed prayer and leave them there to simmer. Cook over med/low heat for two hours, stirring occasionally.

THIS IS TO THAT

Not to Bhishma though he hung upside down in the invisible pit, tangled in vines, refusing to mourn like an ordinary man, not to the five-headed snake who menaced him from below, not to the wild elephant tossing his tusks at the top of the pit, not to wilderness threatening to swallow him, not to the wild bees dropping honey, but to that drop of honey that landed on Bhishma's outstretched finger and was transported trembling to his tongue: Amber tear/labor of bees/blueprint of laughter/rich frosting of Bhishma's breath in winter/nursemaid to raw throats/nectar's plumpest angel/defier of death/sweetness of gravity/astronaut of sugar gliding to earth on parachute silk/latticework of song/siren tempter of taste buds/gloss of deceivers/velvet edge of melancholy/Emily's feathered bird suddenly remembering all the words to hope.

Peter Johnson

VACCINATION, IN THE BROADEST SENSE OF THE TERM

Just as the pharmacist drove the vaccine into my arm, I thought, "So what did you do today, Peter?" I shaved, then looked into the mirror without disappointment, wondering why it took sixty-nine years for that to happen. I had an argument with my wife about a Biblical plague of ants that had overrun her underwear drawer. I killed a huge spider clinging to the inside of the shower curtain, then washed it down the drain. It crawled out so I killed it again. At 10 a.m. I had a headache the size of Bangladesh. At 11 a.m. it was gone, and by noon a woodpecker had an unfortunate encounter with my sliding glass door. I went for a coffee. Argued with a pickup trucker with a nose ring, who taunted me for wearing a mask. I spoke with two monks outside the grocery store about the pitfalls of wrestling with the unexpected. I went home. The woodpecker had regained consciousness, then flown away. The spider was back, so I killed it again. I went to the library, spoke of the failure of trickle-down economics with the janitor. I left. I gave a lecture about hopefulness to a bunch of squirrels sharing a bagel under a Japanese Zelkova tree. I stopped at the pond and watched the baby geese make their stunning debut. I called my wife, told her to hang in there, that the sequel would be much better. She laughed, then said there was huge spider clinging to a picture of me on her nightstand, its thorax eclipsing my face. "It's so big you can see its eyes," she said. I told her to ignore it, it had earned the right to live.

NICE SOCKS

I'm outside the Covid Compassion Center when Jesus arrives. He says, "The hole in the knee of your jeans was merely purchased." Gibberish, of course, but when Jesus talks, you listen. Is it because of the calmness of His voice? The pools of peacefulness in His eyes? I can feel Him reading my mind. It's like a mule kicking me in the back of my head. Hard not to feel sorry for Him in this weather, with cold slush blanketing the pavement, and He's wearing His trademark leather sandals. I take off my shoes and offer Him my woolen socks. He puts them on, re-straps His sandals. "People are just doing the best they can," I say, thinking He's come back to orchestrate the Final Showdown. He looks up, smiles. "Nice socks," He says. "I'm beginning to accept what I cannot change," I say, trying to make a good impression. He looks up again, points to His feet. "Like I said, nice socks."

CRICKETS

Ah, the wild nights of youth when I could get hammered on tequila, then spend all night translating *The Odyssey*. Now just a little iced tea and a marathon of cheerleader horror movies on the Lifetime Channel. It's Halloween in the age of the New Abnormal when I have to peek at kids from a window like a pedophile as they grab candy bars I've placed six inches apart on a cookie sheet. Tonight is our last gasp before another shutdown, before the wheezing and sirens start again, before the squirrels and the birds too dumb to fly south stare hopelessly at us and say, "Just wear masks, assholes." Once, I took a ride in a red MG with the richest girl in town, who loved me whole-hearted-and-souly until she met the richest boy in town. What would the trick-and-treaters make of that? Perhaps it would partly explain why I'm dressed like a scarecrow and toilet-papering my own home, or why, after they're gone, I sit on the back porch, listening to the last remaining crickets protest the night, barely remembering last summer when they'd had the time of their lives.

Richard Jordan

JESUS ON THE RIVER

Sometimes he thinks he should enter the church, but the river holds him, with kingfishers that rattle back and forth across a quiet pool, slate-blue wingtips almost dipping in, more graceful than clergy. From a boulder in the middle of the pool, he can see parishioners go through the doors. They are small from up there, like dolls. Meanwhile, he admires the way a trout faces the current to breathe and consume what's delivered by the flow—that would make a good sermon, he imagines. It's the one he would give.

MACKEREL DAY

It's a mackerel day, my father used to say, when the lighthouse far off on the island disappeared and fog swirled thick and low over the breakwater, my father puffing his cognac pipe tobacco, me wearing his old red baseball cap, the two of us standing on slick rocks threading silver treble hooks with clams, seagulls circling closer and closer, they knew we'd save some bait, with the moan of a ship out there somewhere or maybe a whale, and I'd ask when the lighthouse would come back and flash, *soon*, and my father was always right, and sometimes—often—I still wake at dawn with a taste of salt air tingling my tongue.

WITH FEATHERS

A child balances atop a cedar split-rail fence, blue jay feather in each hand. She stretches arms wide like a tightrope walker. Her father stands nearby, grilling chicken breasts. Pink juices drip onto crackling twigs and charcoal; smoke matches the color of storm clouds rolling fast across the sky. He flips the chicken over, presses with a spatula. Flames shoot up, sizzle fat and skin. The child squints to see beyond the smoke, the clouds. She's been told her mother's always watching from on high. She closes her eyes and hears a whisper, feels a gust of wind. She flaps her arms and rises. This is the moment she could fly away. Instead, she floats down softly to a post. Light raindrops begin to wet her face: her mother's tears, or God's? Her father turns to her and smiles. It's time to go inside. It's time to eat, then sleep. *Yes, those are pretty feathers.* He tucks them into her braids.

Elizabeth Kerlikowske
TABULA RASA

After history and current events, the teacher announces the chalkboard is dirty, but it's just full of echoes of what was written before, cross-hatched with memory. She asks a child to erase it. The long yellow eraser swoops phrases away but leaves dust rearranged into lines that don't mean anything. Stubborn words disappear but not their afterimages. Meanwhile broken pieces of letters sift into the chalk tray like pieces of the globe if it exploded. How quickly forty years disappear. The enchanted day by the river. Blackberry picking. Names written in dust. A child doesn't understand what dust is, that it's more than itself. It's everything, abridged. The board will not be fully clean until an adult goes after it with soapy water. In a swipe: Viet Nam, gone. The dogs, Thor and Loki, gone. Nothing is left but streaks that define this new emptiness. Alphabet ghosts watch above the board. No one should clean a chalkboard so thoroughly that nothing is left.

AT THE 45TH PARALLEL, HALFWAY BETWEEN THE EQUATOR AND THE NORTH POLE

you can look out the kitchen window and see a brown bear shambling down the old railroad bed. Our bears are midsize, like everything here in the middle parallels. Our trees are big but not giant. Our animals are middling, between herons and hummingbirds, voles and white tail deer. Our sunsets are spectacular when another part of the world is burning. We are not obsessed with being first or best. We would like to disappear and live our lives in private, under trees and behind shrubs, surrounded by burning leaf smell and maple syrup. The time between apple blossom and cider we spend outside. Everyone tends a garden, even if they just grow resentment. Morels bloom under leaves, at the base of trees. We sell them by the bushel to the cities. We dress for comfort and warmth; our style of everything is utilitarian. Sometimes it's hot enough to sleep naked; sometimes the cold reaches through the cabin walls into the bed. We prepare for every eventuality with more cord wood, whiskey, a cupboard of canned beans, and an old paint can full of marijuana. We wade in the spring in the spring until our feet freeze. We mate by friends introducing us to friends; we raise our children the way we were raised, with a dash of enlightenment and plenty of flannel. We are not rabid about politics but everyone votes. Potluck and casserole are the names of winter months. Most people can put their hands on at least one snowshoe with no recollection of where its mate went. We accepted the cell phone tower for convenience and privacy, but it's a lie to say we don't miss eavesdropping on the party line. Children can't wait to leave, and grownups can't wait to return home to the smell of woodsmoke that's more than ambience, to mud, hard work, and community. Drab birds, we perch on the 45th parallel, comfortable and content. Always got something to talk about.

Nina Kossman

KHARKIV

I have been waiting for you, who is a stranger to every city and place on earth that you traverse in search of a home, every town and every village you traveled to, every mountain you fell off and every sea in which you drowned. I have been waiting for your return since the day you were born, from the mother who was born here, and she, in turn, was born from the mother who was born here, and the grandmother of your mother, and the grandmother of the grandmother, and on and on, generations of mothers. What took you so long to return? I, the city of your mother's birth, I, the land of your grandparents, I kept a special place for you, your face cast, your body cast, so you'd fit right in; so you'd exclaim, at every street corner, "I remember this!" even though you were not born here, even though you've never been here, even though you were born in that cold capital whose rule we see as the root of all our troubles, and you, who are of the mothers born here, you, who, at a young age, had been taken to live overseas, you returned to me, finally, you have come to the place you belong, where, at every street corner, you meet the self that never lived here, your own self that lay immobile, still, frozen in time for half a century, while you searched for home in many countries, cities, streets, some beautiful, built of sandstone, some so-so, built of depressing red brick, but in all of them you were a stranger, a passer-by, someone without a name, and only here you are at home, because only here, waiting for you, are the graves of your grandmothers (mass graves, in which your grandmothers were buried alive), and only here I, the city you were destined for, am waiting for you. I am your city. I waited for you, since the day your mother was born in my womb; I waited for you, since your day of birth, and even more so, since the day you crossed the ocean to live in the city which had not waited for you and never recognized you, just as you did not recognize it. It was for you I preserved myself, it was for you I stayed beautiful, as though frozen in time, unlike those cities you call ugly and boring (a funny habit you have, don't you think?)—so you would recognize me. So you would love me. So you would welcome me, the way I welcome you, the prodigal daughter, the child I never had. You belong to me. I open myself to you. I show you places no one else has seen. Stay here. Do not leave. You are home.

NOTE LEFT AT A U.S. CAMPTOWN BROTHEL FOR MY MISSING IMO

Dear Sixth Imo, Grandfather's youngest daughter,

No one taught you to write "petal" / unfurling red across the bed / creek cutting the mattress / No one told me your name / chalk to sketch your body starred and open / so Grandmother could buy white rice while the neighbors ate barley / Nobody asked where her money came from / They knew where youngest daughters disappeared to / why their mixed babies disappeared too / what math purchased seaweed for soup fed to the married eldest delivering a son / The first time I heard the rumor of you it was a mistake / to ask your name because Omma wanted to hide you / Just as she hid the fact of me I also hid the words I knew—kijichon, yanggongju, koa, ibyeongah / I hid under the bed, in the cupboard, behind clay pots / all the names for absence feeding our family who chewed and chewed

BUS STOP MATH

It's April 29, Pittsburgh. My skin is on fire, my skin like Bonnie Pham and her son Chris sobbing on the Post-Gazette's front page, "Cold killer's 20-mile trail leaves 5 dead," and as I board the 71C Shadyside to the Pitt campus, I burn like a target among white people reading or daydreaming while plugged into their Walkmans, shoulders slouched against safety glass, legs stretched across the aisles.

I go to the back of the bus among the sleepers. My skin hurts with *What if*? What if Richard Baumhammers boarded this bus and pulled out a gun? Whose skin would become scenery like trees impassive to the forest floor? Whose skin would he gaze past, his grip tightening on the Glock, his line-of-sight tracking?

I do the math: seventeen white women, twelve white men, a Black bus driver, and me. Boarding the bus, Baumhammers would need to spread his arms like a tree—his right hand aimed at the driver, his left at me. I count again: two targets, one tree.

The bus swerves onto Liberty Avenue. My body like a pouch empties out; a wind that's not a voice flaps inside me and hardens a beak. This public space rattles, but I absorb the shock. I swallow the crow that tries to break my throat.

FANTASTIC IMAGINARY CREATURES

When I ask my student whether the plush creature—it's tawny brown, after all, with satin wings—is a sphinx, they bow their head, embarassed. Then they say, *It's a dragon, A copper dragon.* Alex is nonbinary, I think of the one hundred million pennies a copper dragon might hoard, the eighty nine Moscow mule mugs. This is not the first stuffed animal I've seen in a college class. An old girlfriend from when I was their age sends me a page from her old journal in which she describes me as too serious: sphinx-like. "But he's a Leo so he's supposed to be." Explains it all. We were in love, as the saying goes, but that was decades ago. Love, such a chimera. After class, Alex thanks me for not teasing about the dragon, says I'm enigmatic, that I sometimes talk in riddles. I want to disagree but don't. I say nothing. Outside wind blows the dry snow like sand.

HAPPY PIGS

We grew up with stories of happy pigs—the three playing their pipes and drums to celebrate the death of ole Huff and Puff, and Arnold on *Green Acres*, and kind-hearted Wilbur with his spider friend. There were the ones who stayed home, too. The ones who had roast beef. Even in the lone 4H movie they showed in fourth grade, a narrator celebrated the natural relationship between child and piglet. So many joyous sows! So many ecstatic hogs!

But what of those other ebullient porkers: the ones on bacon packages and the ones dancing in neon above the City Barbecue? This pig wears a top hat and laughs, giddy in the scent from the smoker. How lucky he is to have this gig, beckoning us to come with our napkins, our forks and knives.

BAD MEDICINE

Everybody has a little Bon Jovi in them, and they let him out in the car or in the canned goods aisle, the eighty faces of stewed tomatoes watching you like a person possessed, singing and air-guitaring to Living on a Prayer. Well, maybe not everyone, but almost everyone, especially those of us who grew up in the 80s or in New Jersey or who ever once declared to no one in particular that *It's my life* and hoped for power chord roar behind them. I don't even like Bon Jovi, but there he is anyway wanting out. He checks off the women in my past who gave love a bad name, all those times I felt wanted, or simultaneously dead and alive, those times I felt like I'd been shot through the heart and longed for some sort of cure.

Laura Lani

SORRY

i made you so angry my fetus fucked up your party dad tricked you i made you so fat you were too sick to smoke dad dropped you off with your bag full of tricks he left you alone at the hospital you were so scared you tried to escape they caught you on the front stairs the nurse was a rabid raccoon who hissed you'll die if you don't stay still you thought you'd be thin right after i came you cried when you crawled out of bed saw that you were still fat but this story's not funny you had to do everything for me when the nurse was not there there were nine months of diapers an eternity nine months of carrying me i cried when you left me alone a baby's a buzzkill at dinner you needed more time to be free to grow up things aren't how we want them to be

but jesus christ what about me

things aren't how we want them to be you needed more time to be free to grow up a baby's a buzzkill at dinner i cried when you left me alone an eternity nine months of carrying me there were nine months of diapers when the nurse was not there you had to do everything for me but this story's not funny you cried when you crawled out of bed saw that you were still fat you thought you'd be thin right after i came the nurse was a rabid raccoon who hissed you'll die if you don't stay still they caught you on the front stairs you tried to escape you were so scared he left you alone at the hospital dad dropped you off with your bag full of tricks you were too sick to smoke i made you so fat dad tricked you my fetus fucked up your party i made you so angry

Sorry

Joseph Lerner

BLACK EGRET

The trapper follows the creek, wet boots ringing with each step, the sky like an iridium clock. All traps are empty save one, the weir-net strung like jewelry across the creek's neck before it plunges toward the falls.

The trap glints, bulges, a large black egret entangled within. The trapper kneels, slowly extricates the creature, which nips at his hands, drawing blood. He carries it then drooping in his arms back home.

Night has fallen, his wife and children already in bed. Gruel for dinner, a bowl saved for him. Later, lying beside his wife, he hears the egret's cry from the shed where he's confined it, wing broken but on the mend.

His wife also hears and kisses her husband, and draws him nearer her breast. Toward dawn, careful not to wake her, he goes to the shed. The egret, quiet, stirs, lifts its long neck, catches his eye. It will live, he thinks, then shuts the door.

A black egret is a rare thing, saving it good luck. If today his traps are empty, he'll slaughter it, nonetheless. Again he follows the creek, the weir slick with exhalations, with a foul, ravenous light. The falls roar. He stands by the edge.

In the sky, a flock of egrets, hundreds, white and black, tumble, wings glinting, against the sun.

Geri Lipschultz

APHRODITE IN MANHATTAN

Not knowing whether she was feathered eel or leak-sprung boot, he answered the door. She had brought him soup, had chanced to touch his fingers warm as the tongue of a sheep. Now, he was Mars reclining upon the chaise. Behind her the chair where she would sit. And there, his gesture to remove her coat. His eyes scouts for the trembling hand, and the hands, too, are scouts. She has come prepared for this. She plucked her brows and fashioned herself in garments to part the seas. She reads the titles of his scattered books. Part dog and part scientist, she gathers evidence. Finds that what lingers in the trash is more insidious than what clings to a wall. A city ends here, in this room, and in the others cradled within this brick; sadness cooked up and delivered to cluttered caves of solo citizens. These are kingdoms of solitude. Rodin would send Rilke out on missions to explore the panther in its gloom, the sculpture in its dish. Like the current from a dried up stream, she's barely visible, but she has come through a forest of decades to piece him together. His wish? Explore her and then scavenge for the next blue fish.

Lorette C. Luzajic

FEATHERS

Woman, you who never wore a bra, you who never guzzled wine, now have dark birds and their shrouded nest in your tit, swollen stone eggs you thought were nothing until they were something. We were at the brink of gravity when we met, our blooms long spent. Still, we were radiant with that independence of women "coming into their own." Hell's din and swell had dimmed down to a dull roar. The struggle had found formidable and seasoned foe. Well, I watched you carry the skinny drunk chick upstairs from the building backyard, holding your favourite shawl over her wet jeans on behalf of her dignity. I watched you fight like a lion for me when I made a wrong turn, and gave all my love to the wrong man. I took up your flag when a mutual friend you thought could love you, could not love you, after all. It cut us both to pieces. You boiled water until it was hissing spit, tossed tea into the cauldron, mothered my wounds with theophylline and honey. I sheltered you when her door was locked, when things turned mean. We would stake out the city from one end to the other in the caustic cold of February, or hike to Spadina to slurp spicy pork bone soup like starved and frozen explorers. And here we are, now, face to face, after everything, taking on the inevitable. It is now, or it is later, but it is what is. This wild unwinding, this unknown known. Now we await the results of scans, configure charts, see signs in winter flight, in the shrill shudder of fate and her unmoored mutterings. I can't imagine you sick or not there, beg you to stay. You tip your feathers to the wind, say what will be, will be.

JANUARY RIVER

You didn't say much, so I did all the talking. Chattering about my library books or the clues I'd found in the hollow of the dead tree that bridged the creek with your yard. You would wash the dishes, I would dry, and then we would have tea. Black, with a splash of citrus. I loved the flush of youth still round on your leather cheeks, and I loved the old blue and white cups we sipped from. While we waited for the water to boil, I would stand in the corridor and get lost in the Dutch still lifes, reproductions framed in dirty yellow gilt. Like the drapery in winter at the lighthouse, the paintings were heavy and distant, but I was drawn to them. They all said there was more buried in you than were gone in that winter river. I waded through the cracking paint and grime to reach for a bruised apple or a pocket watch in the fading light. I understood that the details of your silence were hidden here, among ruddy crustaceans, skinned lemons, the thin curly rind, ribbon as delicate as paper.

Gary McDowell

PROSE POEM ON THE NATURE OF THINGS; OR, ARMCHAIR PHILOSOPHY

Not knowing the meaning behind something isn't the same as not being able to solve for x. One might be, simply, a lack of academic knowledge; the other is an unwillingness to engage. In my backyard I've inherited a North American Persimmon. When we moved in it was badly overgrown, vined, mossed. I trimmed and culled, cared for and nurtured. Come early fall, the air not crisp, not here, but instead full, expectant, the spice of hot dirt and bug spray, the first reprieve from summer's long seethe, and the fruit drops. The dogs ignore them with their tongues but obsess with their snouts. Tart, bitter, safe: Google tells me not to worry, but in my hands the orange melts, flesh becomes flesh, the sweet, the seeds, the ooze of overripe. I accidentally step on one barefoot. Between my toes like hot milk on the tongue, viscous and unpleasant. Do I rake them up? Do I leave them for the rabbits, the skunks, the fox? Several weeks prior: Dad, dad, dad! There's a fox in the backyard! And there it was, the same color as the fallen fruit, its tail ringed black before it disappeared into the treeline as quickly as it arrived. Fox are my favorite animal, she said. A group of foxes–or is it fox?–are called a leash. I tell her we should set out a bowl of water at the edge of the yard, maybe some table scraps–what do foxes eat? I ask. No, we can't. Because then she will depend on us and won't fend for herself. Sometimes a metaphor speaks for itself immediately, but sometimes you have to be picking the flesh of a persimmon from between your toes for it to hit you: meaning is inherited in much the same way that every child grows up to leave her parents, if we're lucky.

ANOTHER APOCALYPSE

Cloudy with a chance, and there the weatherwoman cuts out.

Radio silence. Dumb silence, or apathy. Everything has types, including types. Nobility is forgetful the same way apprehension is sensory. There's a moat around my mother's house, and if I yodel succinctly, she'll lower it. If I sing slightly off key, the weatherwoman will lower it.

Have you ever watched a blue jay bathe? They ripple. They spout. *This is the force of faith.*

We evolved to commute, my wife says. Out the front window we watch the neighbors pack their two kids into the minivan; the exhaust from the tailpipe pummels the air. It's 16 degrees. Luxury is waking to Eggo's with fresh strawberries and chocolate milk, a warm ride to school. In the dark.

Sober. Fertile. In our current political times, you can only be one.

Farmers use daylight savings time to plant one more acre of soybeans so we can read this morning's news—which includes critiques of daylight savings time—on our doorstep. In the dark.

The leading cause of divorce is marriage.

More than half—53.85% to be exact—of the citizens of Phnom Penh get around via scooter. More than half—99% to be exact—of the citizens of my small town cannot pronounce or locate Phnom Penh on a map. This is not a criticism of small towns; this is a criticism of silence.

An untethered falcon atop the loblolly pine.

My type is one who is breathing, says the former President. And blondes, he adds. And we wonder why we're sick. The grief we carry is older than we are and is far beyond our ruin. It is, instead, an arrival. Cloudy with a chance, she says, for sunlight if you just look hard enough.

Kathleen McGookey

NIGHT SKY WITH CALCULUS WORKSHEET

Like always, the stars are numberless and mute. They can't help you. That glimmer under a closed door might lead to the pool of light cast by a green banker's lamp or a pen scribbling, then swiftly crossing out. Doubt curls in your lap, kneading its paws and purring. Sleep is an elegant, lonely theory. The attic beams creak a little in the wind; the clock ticks late, late, late. Is an axe the inverse of greed? No, axe must equal greed which equals your ancient pine bed, shimmering upstairs like a mirage. In this particular case, bats flock like a physical whisper inside the eaves again. Tonight, one has blundered into the ductwork, and scrabbles now, softly, behind the furnace grate, tapping and tapping to be let out.

DEAR B,

Dear B,

There is an arrow that is not my aim, making for the breast of the world. The left ventricle of my heart, at its odd angle, weeps. At birth, I am not born. The shepherd of my heart leaps among the yellow earth. There is no waking that is not my scream, branching like fire through the bone-dry woods, crying to be nested in the wind. And black death comes with its God cape. And black death comes with its godless mouth. A wafer of darkness will dissolve in the darkness. The rivers are names we say in our sleep. Insects drown out the moon. We live crouched down where an amen in the garden wakes. An amen in the heart's wall weeps. It was the wind that wounded us. It had our shape. It was the bloodhounds that smelled our hunger. Trade winds take us for a windowpane and turn. Death's black tackle in the harbor of the throat. Danger burns its lantern down our barley-darkened hold. Plait of the Lord, let me smolder.

IDENTIFYING THE PATHOGEN

It has its clotted collar, it has extravagant cuffs. It has enough phobias to go sloe-eyed into a slippery past. One only needs to slink like an elm for the joints to crack, for the black roar of rot to come and smoke and love the scar of the trunk. Meats thrum. Pulp. Rust.

One must grow the organism to identify it. Produce the toxins. Predict the dust.

Even the wife of a delicate man is liable to keep the hospital from the house. Even the smells rise up from the treated gauze, even minor wounds are taken seriously. Sanitized of the spore.

The anatomical lab takes a biopsy. The clinical lab takes blood. The lobes of the brain fateful in their sift through liquid fat and blooms of waste. There is a small god in the hooves of their roots. If they do the blood work, they conduct biography. If they do the scrutiny, they give the dose.

What will someday be dead is always unsure.

The quality of the sample is only as good as the news of its results. Fish for a liter of flesh. Weigh it against its porcine core. Wash in vinegar the exposed organs. Jar the liver. Jar the heart.

ANTIDOTE WITH ATTEMPTS AT DIAGNOSIS

They did the test of the body placed beside a flint-skinned nurse, the test for epidemics formed of mirrors, the test of the lethal pills hidden in the eyeglasses.

They did the flow of sodium ions into nerve cells, they did filth in each of the orifices, they did a gem, a pollen shape, they did a transfusion to the vein.

They kept evolving unpredictable results, found a vertigo of snakes and called it the mind, found time and called us its puppets.

They began to sense eternity and accumulate remorse.

They filmed the corrosion each touch would cause, test for hemorrhaging, test for poison, test for the memory of adolescent faith.

They found the secret room where all the genomes drape. They closed a hand's palm made of images over all nomadic sleep.

They found a landscape in the eye, doing its quiet singing.

They mixed situations to administer with the full complexity of weather, mixed the plumage of unmade bones with their gutterless fray, with a thaw as raw as speech, to help them fracture like timbers or a dove's cluttered voice.

They proceeded with medications, experimental embalming, anorexic restoration, therapeutic disturb.

They admitted an inability.

They lost count of the dying. They fished infants from the creek.

They slept in proximity of the mouths of others to be somewhat like breath.

Robert Miltner

HOPELESS

You're pushing a load of clothes into a wash machine at the Suds & Duds Laundromat in Canton, Ohio   Dark socks and boxer shorts   Tees and jeans   That polyester dress shirt you own & don't have to iron because you don't own an iron   Soap   Fabric softener   Four quarters   The first seven months after the divorce   The letter the bounce girl left on the passenger seat of your truck & that you forgot was in the back pocket of your slacks   What you said to the sweet girl from Tallahassee that night you drank too many Irish whiskeys   What dirty things you did   Your embarrassment when the management arrived   More soap   That weekend at the motel in west Cleveland with the party girl flight attendant from Waukegan   The way the room kept spinning   Soap   More bleach   More soap

WOLF DANCING

No way you can stop fox-trotting on the back of a moving fox   Not with its fur red as a Spanish Rioja wine, its tail a frightened dust mop, its ears as pointed as folded French dinner napkins, the zany snout conical as a megaphone   But wait: you pirouette on the xylophone of its spine, hold out your equilibrium arms as if the fox is a small wagon and you're driving a matched team of Belgian draft horses at a small town carnival   But wait: when you look down you realize this isn't a fox: it's a large wolf, a dark nocturnal canine disguising itself as a vixen   But wait: it begins to transform again: it becomes a gray Irish wolfhound   A red Irish setter   A red wheelbarrow   What's next: a crayon-yellow cheetah or an ocelot?   No way you can suppress your joy at Disco dancing on the back of a racing wolf   No way you can catch your breath break dancing at sixty miles an hour on the back of a rapid animal that answers to no name

HULA DANCER

She will dislocate her hips. Or maybe they're already dislocated, a kind of double-jointedness, like the suburban girls back East who wrap their heels behind heads in slumber party stunts. There is fury in her rhythm, her belly a dark blur beneath coconut c-cups. More than once a drunk man in an airport aloha shirt has slipped a hotel key in the cinched waist of her grass skirt, slurring a room number in her ear. She drops the keys in the trash with the paper plates from this nightly luau staged by a fair-skinned businessman from Chicago. After the show, she'll change into a tank top and low-rise jeans with a red thong peeking up in back. She'll board the number 8 bus—named, after a decade of *island time* planning, simply *The Bus*—and listen to Ludicrus on her iPod as she makes her way inland to neighborhoods where laundry stretches across apartment balconies. On Monday, her night off, she'll sit with a bottle of Sunny Delight under a line of dishtowels and her father's boxers as the wind picks up, lifting the clothes, bending the palms. And in between the buildings, pulsing low and steady, she'll see the real sun, Victoria's Secret red, right where it belongs.

GERUNDING

When Mad Libs had blanks for gerunds instead of dumbed-down *-ing* verbs, we caressed wood pulp paper with pencils, erasing our answers to play again and again, *stroking* becoming *licking* becoming *sucking* becoming *fucking*, you becoming a junior whose boyfriend dies cheating, drowning after careening drunk into a flooded creek, the other girl escaping, you learning to fall in love with the pain.

EKPHRASIS

When my parents split, he got the projector and she got the slides. Now both are mine. On our living room wall, I meet my college-girl mother in black & white: swept-up hair, unfiltered smile. *Shot through the lens of love*, my husband assumes. Perhaps. But I know my father loved gadgets—he was likely swooning over f-stops and shutter drag. And here I am, unprepared for sole custody of their past.

DECADE

I sit on the pool's edge and watch my daughter swim. She dives underwater then surfaces beside me. "Momma," she says, "I was trying to see how long I could hold my breath…what it would be like to drown but couldn't. I popped up for air."

I kiss the top of her swim cap. "Your body has instincts. It will fight to breathe. It wants you to stay alive."

*

I am behind and need to get ahead. Too tired for both/either. My children need me, the dogs and cats need me, and the soon-to-be-ex-husband has equal need, too. No purposeful efficiency. Drivel scribble.

*

Therapist: "Imagine your future writing space."

Oratorical pitch against suicide! We imagine! and by imagining, stretch forward a proposal! make an offering to some future self. *What I believe can/will be*. I dare not. *Who the fuck cares* if I write another word? I don't. But I *do*… so I write about my walk to the lake and tall grass brushing my cheeks and dragonflies and damselflies flitting around and the hawk slow-circling high above the pines, carving its path through the sky with tilted wings as if writing itself into being.

*

Late night student email: leave of absence, bulimia, hospitalization. *Please don't worry about class*, I write. *Make up missed work whenever you're ready.* What I want to write, but don't? *How courageous. I can't speak of my own fucked up suffering with anyone.* (On this night, after starving all day? My own post-haste post-dinner vomiting. Buhbye Pasta Bolognese. *Less of me*.)

*

Therapist waits for me to speak.

Me, finally: "It's not that I'm not okay, it's that I'm not here— a moth thumping at the window. The light over there, on the other side. I'm over here in the dark outside."

*

"I'm reading! I'm really reading!" My daughter in ecstasy—sounds into words, words into sentences, the sum total shouted out with glee. "Momma! Help me!" I delay. With each word she gets on her own? *If... I... had... a... dragon...* inky lines and curlicues cartwheel across the page, down the stairs, out the door, and into the world. When I finally go upstairs to her bedroom? She is wide-eyed, otherworldly, ravenous. Books surround her on the bed. Radiant plunder.

*

Life-sized stuffed tiger in psychiatrist's waiting room. At its feet, a bin of mangled toys. Stuffed animals—parrot, cat, whale, unicorn—and plastic babies missing limbs and eyes and clumps of hair. A warning taped to the wall: *For Your Safety Please Do Not Sit on the Tiger.* A test? Transgress and sit on the tiger? I open a *Highlights* magazine. Hidden Picture puzzle. *Can you find: pencil, fishhook, candle, and axe? Can you find: DSM code, Rx, cure, and miracle? Can you find: your way back?*

*

The backroad, the long way home, twice as long in snow, was necessary: enough time to finish the argument started in the therapist's office.

"We have our separate secret longings," she says.

"And still we don't know what we want," he says.

*

My son tapes paper scraps together, then draws pictures, and rushes to find me. "Momma, you write my story," he pleads. I stop unloading the dishwasher, stop folding laundry, stop vacuuming, put away whatever it is that I am doing. He whips out sentences so fast I can't keep up—witches, werewolves, and walks through dark forests—then begs me to read his story again and again. He knows the plot but that linear progression of letters that are words that are written story surprise him each time—*mine, me, here*!

*

Therapist: "My brother died today. I hate funerals. Promise me that you'll live."

Me: "I'll try."

Therapist: "Will. Live. Will. Say Yes."

*

My son reads aloud from his one-hundred+ page story, *The Dark Lands*: "There's solid memory and there's liquid memory." He does not elaborate.

*

The world outside is hard; the world inside, too.

But also: we go for a backroads drive. I stop the car over and again to watch the world reveal itself: deer flash then freeze then disappear into the woods; horses in a pasture amble over to the fence and nicker and huff; a stray cat rubs itself around my daughter's legs; my son is impatient with the sun's slow setting though I am not. I feel how we carry our years, our lost and found selves--sometimes in secret, sometimes in the open.

Remember. Yes. Write this down.

Robert Perchan

THE ORGUN BOX JUNKIES

One summer afternoon my family took delivery of the first Orgun on our block. It arrived inside an Orgun Box but the Orgun was soon removed from the Orgun Box and installed in our parlor. The Orgun Box itself was set out by the curb to be admired by the neighborhood. As each kid climbed in and came out drenched with envy I discovered I was loathed as never before. Bicycles pedaled by and slowed down in front of the Orgun Box. Then they leaned forward and sped off. Soon the street and then the whole town was littered with Orgun Boxes on all the curbs. But now the envy and hatred was transfigured into fellow feeling and a sacred kind of love none of us kids had ever known before. Not an Orgun Box was empty of us kids all throughout the day and deep into the night as our parents danced in their parlors to their Orguns and its tunes. This rapture lasted until the Orguns in our parlors began to sort of grind inside and fire blanks. First only one blank in maybe a thousand notes and just the occasional grind. Then no less than one blank in a hundred and a likewise grind. My Dad took ours apart and oiled it and snapped it back together but that only made it worse. Soon enough it was firing one blank in every ten notes. Then things got really bad. Till every other note was a blank and then nothing but blanks and nothing but grinds. What, Dad said, was the point. Look at all these blank notes lying around. And listen to those grinds. This wasn't part of the deal. That nightfall we uninstalled the Orgun from our parlor and wheeled it out to the curb and pushed it inside the Orgun Box. And the rest of the dutiful town followed suit. The next afternoon the Orgun Boxes were loaded on trucks with Hats and Flat Shoes at the wheel. We were asked to sign pledges that said No, we had never touched the Orguns at all. No, they had been delivered by mistake. We were not ready for them yet. No, it had been an experiment. The Orguns were not good for us after all. No, they were flawed. If the Orguns were misused we might hurt ourselves. What about, we cried, the fellow feeling and the sacred kind of love none of us kids had ever known before. The rapture. Did you really feel that and know it too, said the Hats and Flat Shoes. Are you sure. Yes, we cried. Yes we felt it and we knew it too. Well, said the Hats and Flat Shoes, can you wear a red cap and a bellhop jacket with gold braid. Yes, we cried. Yes we can. And can you hold a tin cup and dance to a grind. Yes, we cried. Yes we can. Take us with you.

And they did and we do.

THE UNSELFISH ELFINS WITH THEIR TRUSTY HAMMERS

They were a wondrous and crafty folk. Anything I could come up with in words, they seized with their tongs and hammered out at their forges. Aeroplane nectar. Clairvoyant brassieres. Bucolic steel. So I set them to work on humanity's highest aspiration, her noblest project: Nature without Predation. Soon the queues at the meat counters thinned, and vanished. People still cruised and chatted one another up, though with a curious lack of resolve. At Mi Casa or Tu Casa they pieced together jigsaw puzzles on the satiny bedsheets. Watchtower cartoons of gentle lions lying down in a sea of lemmings. On topless tropical beaches bathers cuddled tentacled jellyfish against their hairy chests: "Look, Muriel! I've got jiggly jugs—just like you!" In the icy chambers of the deep rogue great whites shed their sandpaper skin and abjured their rapacious ways, their pitiless opaque gaze softening to a merry twinkle. On leafy twigs green Mrs. Mantis deigned not to dine on the proffered head of green Mr. Mantis and copulation muted to a serene evening of companionable prayer. Amoebas, under the microscope, bounced jollily off their prey like colored balloons at a birthday party. Even sullen serial killers in Kiev, in Boston, in Brisbane, in Kuala Lumpur turned out to be garrulous backslappers at heart after all. Me, unable to contain my joy, I wandered out into the repristinated night to marvel at the rival stars, which had ceased to feast on one another, which had ceased to burn.

AT HOME WITH MARLBORO JONES

A soft, snowy day in early spring so I put my heavy-duty books on my feet and walk out into the yard. My wife watches me from the window above the kitchen sink. It was she who put my books by the front door and my boots on the bookshelf. She knows the neighbors will call the men in the white lab coats that nobody can see because they are white against a perfectly snowy day. Until they arrive I will tramp around the yard in my books. The pages are white with little black specks on them like the faeces of some tiny critter with an absolute genius of a sphincter. *It was a bright cold day in April, and the clocks were striking thirteen.* If you think that's crazy you should see my wife taking down my boot from the bookshelf and sticking her nose in it. Maybe she's doing it just for kicks. Have you ever read a book that was like a boot to the face? It's called *1984*. Something about a boot stomping on human faeces. If you think that's crazy well if *face* isn't the English singular of the Latin plural *faeces* I don't know what is. If you think that's crazy did I mention I am walking through the white pages of *1984* while I wait for the men in white coats to arrive that I will never see until they are upon me. If you think that's crazy did I mention how I know I will never hear *Wipe your books before you come back in again.* If you think that's crazy did I mention it's a soft, snowy day and I am writing all this right now on the white walls of my padded room. In faeces, natch. But human ones.

THE CELL

Don't worry about getting up this morning and finding yourself alone. You are not expecting anyone. It's okay to sit in the dusk and take in the emptiness from the imagined shelves filled with books against these walls, and it's only you in the filthy reflection of the window. No one is coming for you today, or tomorrow most likely. The room and you are almost one entity, giving life to each other, or so it must seem. You don't have to cry out for anyone because nobody will come. Now and any other time of day or at any given moment in your life, there is only you and your thoughts. Go ahead, put your arms around yourself, feel yourself until there is nothing left but your heartbeat in your ears.

TO GABRIELA, IN MEMORY

I wipe my greasy fingerprints from my roommate's aquarium as the stupid goldfish blows kisses at me, before I shut the door to my dormitory and abandon my coffee-stained desk and warped wooden bookcase; I turn off the light and remember my sister. She's in the kitchen, her bunny slippers with their plastic eyes and floppy ears guiding her to me. She carried a lime-green acrylic sweater, a handful of ripe fruit—a going away present. Her kisses like those Father Pedro would give on Saturdays after confessional when I was eight. My tears and snot melted into my mouth drowning out my voice before the Hail Mary's and Our Father's absolved me of stealing Doña Virginia's oranges. And in that instant, I thought I almost heard her cry for me to leave the light on, afraid to go to sleep in the darkness half a world away.

Christine Rhein

DRONE PILOT

He changes into his flight suit, goes to war each morning—just a twenty-minute drive from Vegas, his wife and kids. He doesn't talk much about the base, the windowless days, trapped smells of coffee, candy, sweat. In a darkened room: six glowing screens, joystick, throttle, the padded chair. He rubs his neck as if to unknot dangers he knows can't ever reach him. Sometimes he holds his breath as he centers the crosshairs over a rooftop, waits for the countdown, for the missile to hit, the smoke to flow, keep flowing. The AC hums. The chair tilts back. With hands at rest on the metal console, cold switches, he feels the fear of striking a child or a good guy. For a moment, he closes his eyes, pictures the concrete rubble crushing his own body, his face. Shift in, shift out, no logging off, no putting the power to sleep.

No putting the power to sleep, no logging off. Shift in, shift out, rubble crushing his own body, his face. The concrete pictures—he closes his eyes. For a moment, he feels the fear of striking a child or a good guy with hands at rest. On the metal console—cold switches. The chair tilts back. The AC hums: keep flowing. For the missile to hit, the smoke to flow, the countdown waits. As he centers the crosshairs over a rooftop, dangers he knows can't ever reach him, he holds his breath. Sometimes he rubs his neck as if to unknot the padded chair, six glowing screens, joystick, throttle, sweat. In a darkened room, trapped smells of coffee, candy, the windowless days, the base. He doesn't talk much about his wife and kids, Vegas just a twenty-minute drive each morning. He changes into his flight suit, goes to war.

SUNDAY NIGHT, RETAIL

—Lisa, Impact Team Member

They tell me to be creative in this job. And detail-oriented too. Even way past closing—doors locked, lights low. I'm stuck with cotton T's and folding time, refolding time—fluff, stretch, crease—rectangles matched and stacked into neat invitations: "Dear Shopper, Please touch and dig through all the colors. Lavender. Daffodil. Sweetest Lime." Spring launch is a dream. Or a great big joke. It's February. Doesn't Corporate know anything about Chicago, all the slush I mop away? Fluff. Stretch. Crease, crease, crease. They tell me there's an art to meeting quota, sales coming down to eye contact, smiles. It's work. And more than work. And just me here, alone, smoothing out a hem, spreading out a chest, hiding the sleeves—one, two—empty arms.

Lee Ann Roripaugh

NOTES ON DISSOCIATION

The summer comes unbuttoned and your mind slips free of its body to float up and nudge the corner of the ceiling like a Mylar balloon: *happy birthday! happy birthday! happy birthday!*

Sulky with poison rain, you're a swollen cloud casting shadows over the plains. What would happen if you were to pour yourself out onto that ground, until everything darkened, until everything was all shadow?

Your body dreams of invisibility: like January black-out fog muffling the headlamps of your car on I-29 as the river exhales its thick clouds of icy breath.

Your body dreams of camouflage: an effervescent fizz into gray television static.

The summer comes unbuttoned. The pandemic surges and wanes. Children killed in mass shootings. Unarmed Black bodies martyred by the gunfire of police officers in state-sanctioned lynchings during routine traffic stops. The bodies of Asian women murdered. The bodies of Asian elders assaulted in the streets.

Your Japanese mother, on lockdown in Memory Care nine hours away, tells you she hates you before hanging up the phone.

(It doesn't particularly matter which summer's the summer that comes unbuttoned because isn't this *any* summer, anymore?)

Dissociate: as in a social severing. A breakup, a friendship's end, a professional splitting of ties. How your parents sever you off like a cancer, even though you're their only family. How they refuse to speak to you until they need your help. And because you're the only one left, you must return to parent the parents who were not good parents to you.

(With your feet on the air / and your head on the ground / Try this trick and spin it, yeah / Your head will collapse / If there's nothing in it / And you'll ask yourself / Where is my mind?)

The first time the summer comes unbuttoned you're molested by the boy who lives across the street. He says he's doing what he's doing to you because you're *half Japanese*. Your parents say it's *your* fault he does what he does to you because you don't make him *show* you the gun he points at you from inside his windbreaker. How the boy isn't really a boy. He is 18. You are 8.

You think about the very word, *trigger*: how it brings to mind bullets, how it brings to mind the permeability of bodies, both physically and psychologically.

You think the unbuttoning has something to do with the *nonconsensuality* of it all. Of the *rapey-ness* of the anti-maskers and the anti-vaxxers. Of the *rapey-ness* of the shooters. Of the *rapey-ness* of the rapists.

When that panicked feeling of being trapped inside some meat-sack of disaster comes, why wouldn't you want to be somewhere / anywhere else?

Dissociation: for you, the *flight* of fight or flight. Nowhere for the body to go to feel safe. Hatchet out an escape hatch, quietly slip out of the lid. Like Elizabeth Bishop's Man-Moth, who "thinks the moon is a small hole at the top of the sky, proving the sky quite useless for protection."

(With your feet on the air / and your head on the ground / Try this trick and spin it, yeah / Your head will collapse / If there's nothing in it / And you'll ask yourself / Where is my mind?)

The summer comes unbuttoned and you blow your own mind like a shotgun blast of breath to the head of a dandelion gone to seed. Each seed a tiny parachute spoked with delicate filaments arranged to create a detached vortex when the seed's borne aloft into air. The vortices ferrying the seeds up to half a mile away from the parent plant.

Your body dreams of dispersal: an accident involving teleportation, and now you're a ghost in the machine.

Your body dreams of evaporation: like the spider suspended in medias res, desiccating in the cloudy film of lint behind the dryer.

You think of the sea slug, the Sarcoglossan, also known as the leaf sheep, or the green thief, because it steals chloroplasts from algae and can perform photosynthesis in a daring bank robber-esque move known as kleptoplasty.

You think of how, during extreme duress, certain species of Sarcoglossan can detach their own heads, leave their bodies behind.

(As decoy? As sacrifice? Like dumping out the non-essentials when rutted in mud on the Oregon Trail?)

The decapitated body can live without its head for days, sometimes even months.

If the green thief's young and healthy, the open wound on the back of its head heals, despite its severing intentions, and within days, the head begins to regenerate a new body: a new beating heart, new vital organs. After three weeks, a near-perfect replica of its original body.

But what to do with a discarded body that's absent a head?

(Perhaps you will disguise the headlessness with a mask, the way the Pokémon Cubone wears its dead mother's skull like a fetish for grief.)

The summer comes unbuttoned and your mind blossoms away from your body like a pyrocumulonimbus cloud fueled by wildfires in the American West: fire-breathing, toxic, explosive.

Your body is having nightmares: spiraling fire whirls, flash points, trees crowned in flame.

Your body dreads scorched earth.

But only in scorched earth can you begin to dream again of ephemerals, weeds, the slow march back of wood-boring beetles. Of grasses and scrub. Of birds and armadillos come in search of the beetles. Of raccoons and foxes to curl into hollowed-out wood. Of scrubby canopy to lay down needles and leaves for mulch. Of taller and taller trees. Of vines. Of being nudged by the rough tongues of deer. Of being drenched by a cold hard rain.

Jane Satterfield

ABBREVIATED INVENTORY

You wanted to paint regret? Start by stretching the canvas, lashing raw fabric to frame in whose corners you hammer keys to keep the stretchers flat—think *passé-partout, picture-mounting* or those dense passages in Derrida you tried to read, cold-stunned, over cups of java one winter, snow unleashed in the sky. *Passé-partout, picture-mounting,* as if a single text were a pass-key, *allowing passage everywhere—*. Think of the canvas you bought, sold by the foot, the tips you picked up for priming—how sandpaper on priming strips gloss away, how slash and burn has its appeal; how ground glass gives the pigment something to grip. And what of the ways you prefer your lacunae?—Think of the loggers in that crack-spined novel you've read—the pre-dawn glamour of a lanterned procession, their *axes banging into cold wood as if into metal*. The creek with its water, *molecular and grey*. No matter if the light, the surface, or the canvas fails; no matter the mood, the ordinary sky. No blinding gold light, no fluid blues—no cobalt, federal, midnight. No Prussian, no powder, no steel. You could curry favor with some kind of belief, stand at the window while day plummets to dusk—in whatever pause, whatever transition, whatever future unspooling— *whelk, slipper snail, last leaf on a tree*—you would still have your heart. That conflagration.

Italicized phrases borrowed from: Jacques Derrida, Michael Ondaatje, Beth Kephart.

LATIN 121

8:01 and the class launched into *Pater noster*, centuries sliding away into ablative and genitive, those lessons: syntax as command and control—like learning the stars, the way shape can be slung over infinite skies. What was I thinking that first college year, dark heart wanting to disappear—*punish the body to save the soul?* How I loved nothing more than I loved to translate, as if to crawl into the sorrow, the script where insults and kisses lived on beyond time. Clock ticking. Centuries sliding away…gather a self and dress for the day. Two decades on it's 8:01; my daughter's outside gathering the autumn's first leaves. Anti-aging serum spills into the sink. What do I think I can buy here and now, a lover's cursory kiss, some "operatic grandeur"? Clocking ticking, the senses heightened by hunger. *Salve. Pater.* I stepped out of the classroom back into sunlight, the day auric, emblazoned. Our skewered verse in chalk on the board, riding the current of time.

Katherine Smith

CROSSWORD

It made me happy all day yesterday to know the Marianas Trench was the deepest place on earth, seven miles under the ocean floor, deeper than Mount Everest is high. But not as happy as today, when two down was okapi, a near relative of the giraffe with zebra stripes on its hindquarters and a dark chocolate coat like velvet. The okapi's hooves drip a tar-like substance through the Congolese jungle where it walks in circles all day, eating leaves and guano. And though it looks like a herd animal, lives in complete solitude except for its brief mating, and for a year afterwards with its mother until the baby okapi also learns, like us, to amuse itself in the jungle.

QUILT

In the field across the street from my house, vultures settle on the animal that calls them forth. From every direction they come, gliding over the horizon from their roosts. Death calls them to the feast. Vultures yank ligament, loosen muscle from cartilage with a jerk of wing and shoulder blade. They stretch ribbons of intestines between beak and claw. That was yesterday. This morning, the bones jut, picked clean from antlers to femurs, dragged across the road to the dogwood. At dawn the sun pierces fog, and, on the lawn, the ribs gleam. Near the window, my portion of my mother's ashes still sits on the shelf, enclosed in black ceramic. One day, not yet, I will scatter them in the Chesapeake Bay. Vultures craft a quilt of bone, their hunger and the dead buck stitched together like cotton blocks to backing. One of your names is necessity, your power at work in this world.

YELLOW

I'm wearing my yellow robe, drinking coffee out of a yellow mug that has a rooster on it. When I take coffee into my mouth, I hold off from swallowing and let my tongue believe it's taking a luxurious bath. Traffic swooshes down the street. People are busy being busy. For hours, I've been planning a trip to the end of the driveway to pick up the newspaper. Ravens bicker with each other out in the yard. The cats circle my chair, beg to be let out to murder. Each day we inch our way toward death. One day, without knowing it, we buy the clothes we'll be buried in. We smile for a camera that snaps the shot that'll be used for our obituary. I'll probably die in this robe, but until then I'm going to eat some waffles that come in a box that's also yellow. Often, when children draw the sun, they'll either use a yellow or orange crayon. The older, more advanced children will use both. In kindergarten, there was this kid who drew his suns in big, blood-red circles. The teacher once asked him why he chose red for his suns, and he said, "This is how I see it. This is how it is in my world."

BOOK OF LOVE

The love my partner and I share is a book we've read many times. The pages yellowed. Spine broken. No dog ears, but plenty of bat wings. There's a coffee ring on the cover, and the phone number to a defunct laundromat scribbled below the final paragraph on the last page. It's a story most would find dull. Critics have pointed out its lack of narrative arc. We picked it up years ago at a used bookstore for half-price. She ripped out the page revealing the murderer, so we'd always keep guessing, and to distinguish our copy from all the others, I drew a mustache and devil horns on the author's photo with a red pen.

Virgil Suárez

CHINESE WEATHER BALLOON

Plenty of room in this country for a lost weather balloon, silver and glowing in the blue stratosphere but visible if you squint long enough and your eyes water. Force majeure. Easy to let the currents carry you, weightless like the feeling you get in a rollercoaster free fall. Spy balloon my ass. This one was a birthday gift for a child alien from a distant galaxy whose father promised a trip to Disneyland. On course, the child let it slip and now it hangs over Montana, then Kansas. Adrift and rudderless. Amerikans demand it be shot down and it eventually is eight miles off the coast of South Carolina. So much anticipation and deflation. A dead and bloated jellyfish on the surface of the Atlantic. What is a poet to do but write to a friend to say next time a Chinese weather balloon floats overhead, he will shoot it down and make a dress and matching crown with its luminous material. All of this to tell you I am learning how to sew.

A HUNDRED BIRDS

After her stroke my grandmother lost her sense of taste. Pecked at her food like a sparrow. A cracker became a drawn-out snack. A cube of cheese, a feast. No more chocolate bars in her kitchen drawer. No cheese-puff can on the night stand. She grew thinner, until old pictures looked like someone else: as if *Grandma Kate* were a role played now by a different actress. At first she also couldn't speak. Then learned again, slowly, though names of things escaped her. Sequences. Causes and effects. Why a metal pan couldn't go in the microwave. Why we threw away plastic forks, but not silverware. She chewed her lip. Looked worried, lost. My great aunt's story was different. Once the older sister with her make-up always on, everything just so. A fancy pin closed the collar of her mauve blouse, which matched her skirt and shoes and purse. She made her strongest statements with silence. But after her stroke she became coarse. Aunt June cursed. As if drunk. As if liberating a lifetime of pent-up anger. Call it rage. Yes, but also glee. She giggled. No, cackled—her head thrown back so you could see the pink inside her mouth. Gales of laughter, shits and *sons-of-bitches* flying free. The way a gunshot sends a hundred birds exploding out, when you thought it was an empty tree.

HOW IT STARTS

—To Preston

Too cloudy now to see the stars? At birth they see the face of God, but children soon forget. A crow calls like a mirror: *Crow! Crow!* And finally, that's enough worry: these paths do cross if you follow one far enough. The crow sits high in the pine: purple-black, dense as felt. If only you could remember the first time you looked up at that odd sound and knew: *That's my name.* For a moment, only this world. Maybe this *is* how it starts. Too quickly, before you can think it through, a door swings open. It's the way you narrow your eyes at that sudden glare: a white sheet rippling. How it tugs the line, pulls in light like a window, a bright fish, hope or wish, darting bird, new nail, a coin found on the ground and then just a sheet again. Quiet, now, listen: *Yi bai sui*, Po used to say—now Mama says—when you'd sneeze. *May you live for one hundred years*, starting when you open your eyes.

MY BLINDNESS

Once I woke up in the dark and thought I was blind. There was no light at all. There's always *some* light.

Blind, I was calm in that perfect dark. Friends would come, and I'd tell them what they had to do. It would be all right.

I'd go back home, but *dignified*, and I'd know my way perfectly in the house, even on the streets. I'd only been gone a few years.

I'd have them read me strange books, and they'd love my strangeness, thinking *this is what it was, we knew there was something.* They'd loved it a little already.

There at home in my great dark I'd find a single purpose, and begin.

But you know this: the light came.

Don't laugh at me. I live with so little blindness. Such a long way I've come. So little blindness.

Pat Valdata

MAYFLY

Lilian Bland (1878–1971), first woman to build and fly her own airplane, September 1910

Ash wood, light and strong, is best for spars and skids, but an old bicycle handle will suffice for steering by Carnmoney Hill, where the wind blows steady. Dimensions and measurements are done and dusted, engine fetched by myself from England. Formalin/gelatin soak gives the muslin fabric a good, waterproof coat, ready for the first gliding trial. Horsepower calculated—I needed twenty to attain any height—but would she bear its heft? Irish Constabulary boys (four of them) plus Joe Blaine, my aunt's gardening assistant, provided just what we needed. Knowing the wings would support the engine's weight was a load off. Lord O'Neill offered his acres for takeoff and landing Mayfly, so named because she may fly—or she may not! Noisy engine installed, sorry for the fright, neighbors. Overalls? Oh, with so much oil, a skirt is out of the question. Pull the propellor, Joe, and I'll fly the airplane, one quarter-mile after the rains finally relent. Rise, rise, little Mayfly! Speed enough to progress, albeit slowly, thirty feet we rise above pastures, past the trees, up, where naysayers thought no woman would go unaided. Victory even though every single nut loosened from vibration, even with wires supporting all twenty-seven feet, seven inches of wing. Wires crossed in an X for strength, stretched taut to lessen the yaw. Yes, she flew, and I built her all by myself, indeed yes. Next? Zipping down the lanes in a Ford Model-T, my newest adventure.

SIDESHOW, BARBOUR COUNTY FAIRGROUNDS, 1975

The field under the tent undulated, but it was the bullhorn insistence of the carnival barker that made my stomach burble and turned my tongue to copper: *Come see the Frog-faced Baby, the human baby with the face of a frog!* There was a garish poster of a boy, normal from the neck down but with a bullfrog's head: drawn lips, external eardrum, yellow bubble eyes. *His parents took LSD! Only one dollar to see the Frog-faced baby, the human baby...* the barker continuing his refrain without ever reaching the coda. I don't know why I went inside. It was only a dollar. I was nine years old.

Inside was a different story: preserved in an apothecary jar was a human child, a stillborn baby boy, distended eyes and downturned mouth distorted and magnified by the liquid and curved walls of the jar. I kept looking back and forth between my own hands and his tiny, wrinkled hands under glass. I knew this was something I shouldn't see and yet I walked all the way around him, like you were supposed to, before leaving the tent almost reluctantly, trading my shame for the August heat and the sound of normal, living children, screaming with delight.

TO JOIN THE CIRCUS

He was fifteen years old when he ran off, as people do, to join the circus. His mother wept for two whole days—starved for news—until a postcard came, telling her which train would deliver his dirty laundry for her to wash. She caught the bag at the siding in Hundred, WV on Saturday afternoon, and handed back clean clothes to her grinning son when the circus train slowed for the crossing Monday morning. He'd joined *The Lief Brothers Circus*, out of Fairmont—the local ticket to a life under canvas—and home for church every third Sunday. He started out sweeping the show ponies' stalls, laying down hay after the evening performances and picking up their shit in the morning. He graduated to the show's only elephant, then—little by little—learned tumbling, balance tricks and finally the contortionist's art: passing his slender frame through an unstrung tennis racket or balancing a glass of water on his forehead, lowering himself prone and then getting back to his feet, all without spilling a drop. This was before the war, the first one, the big one, the fields of Flanders and the weeks standing ankle deep in piss and muddy water. The circus had prepared him for that much at least. That and the endless hours of waiting.

OBJECT IMPERMANENCE

>*—After Elizabeth Bishop's paintings*

>"It's big enough so that if you like any section of it, you can cut that part out."
>*—from Bishop's letter to Amy Baumann regarding the painting* Brazilian Landscape

I want to float when I look at these images or at least tilt my head. Even the buildings seem to lack foundations, as if they might list off a hill and drop into a sea no matter how many lines and cords and wires appear to tether the parts together. Windows, portholes, doors, and gravestones lean slightly off kilter. Rather than marking birth or death dates, the inscriptions read "for sale" as if tomb stones could be carried off in armloads. They're propped up against a building rather than sunk in the ground. I could pluck a frame from the wall or pick a rock up and put each somewhere else. Even a body in repose on a bed looks like a paper doll that could be moved to another room or dressed in different clothes. A picture otherwise pins a moment down. But the door opens to a wall of garden as if to say nothing is easily navigated. You are not where you think. Portals are as unpredictable as knob and tube wiring. Scenes expose the volta, what we can only guess at or hope for, the constant drift. As spectator, I'm on my back in the ocean, all sound muffled in my ears to a vague hushed roar. Close my eyes, I'm here by the buoy. Open them, I'm down the shore by the pier. Still life is movable. Something translates desk and table, bouquets in vases, the flowers spilling over under gravity's pull. Some say she didn't consider her paintings art, but I bet she did. Porthole. Tomb. Door. From this to that. What is here, even when we can no longer know it with certainty, the way clouds swallow a full moon, how a simple word whispered from ear to ear soon means something else.

FUGUE STATE

She plays in the key of forgetting. Forgetting, she loses locale, landmarks. Landmarks wander in her mind. Her mind becomes an antic character. An antic character will wonder. Wonder is the destination, unmapped. Unmapped, her trip takes an unexpected turn. Turn loops past the gas station & church. Church reminds her of repentance, an altar. An altar takes shape in her mind like matter. Matter becomes quark, atom, & particle. Particle reminds her of clavicle. Clavicle curves, a bone at the base of throat. Throat opens to voice & air & words. Words may lie because nothing is as it seems. It seems that she is losing her mind. Her mind rounds a corner and runs into a door. A door swings, creaking, hinges into the cerebellum. The cerebellum rests under occipital & temporal. Temporal suggests time, which the eye meets, open. Open, she tiptoes in the vestibular corridors, hearing chimes. Chimes say the clock strikes down the hall. The hall is the vestibule where she waits for language. Language bears the thrum that she cups in her hands. Her hands open & memories fly out like birds. Birds always know where they are going. Going, she hangs her sorrows on a hook in the hall where they jangle, like keys, until she returns.

WHY I LIVE IN A COLD CLIMATE

Because the sound of ice breaking beneath my feet reminds me of wooden ships slowly awakening for a journey. Because that journey can be long and arduous. Because frost collecting in the corners of darkened window glass becomes a kind of map, more reliable than starlight alone. Because I always liked you in a hat, and our bodies draw sudden sparks beneath the drab woolen blankets. Because our breath here can be seen as easily as any cloud passing, our silence sent skyward along with our prayers. Because in winter we walk easily upon water, never questioning the river's current or where we might have left the shore. Because you can follow the tracks of those who have trudged through the snow before you, making a path for others. Because sound travels far in the cold, and we have learned to listen. Because the cardinals and house finches remind us to sing, in spite of it all. Because there are as many names and varieties of snow as there are for their creator. Because whenever you drop a glove here, a stranger will inevitably call out, saving you yet again, and your saying thank you is really an offering of love you cannot quite admit to. But you feel the warmth of that fabric once again encircling your fingers, small but undeniable, feel the pinprick ache of blood's slow and knowing return, and that may be enough for now.

Cathy Wittmeyer

MAX BECKMAN, *STILL LIVE WITH FALLEN CANDLES*, OIL ON CANVAS, 1929

These candles tipped over when the server set down the lopsided stack of silver cheese-&-sweets trays on the wooden stand with the leftover fruit. Nobody cared for the decorative grapes still-on-the-leafy-vine or for the yellow-green pears—the sugar too fleeting on the tongue. Droopy snowbells fleck the taupe wallpaper on repeat—like this insufferable 90s song in my head. You hear it too? One candle burns, so while the stack is ignored, it will flame to nothing but a wisp of paraffin smoke that no one notices because they have all left the dining room, leaving these dishes for the morning shift when even the staff has slept off most of their hangover. The grapes will be wrinkled by then, consigned with the pears to the compost heap to turn into schnapps & intoxicate the crows. Listen, you can hear those black-feathered beasts grousing: *All Good Things Come to an End.*

OTTO DIX, *HORSE CADAVER*, ETCHING & DRYPOINT, 1924

A horse is never just a horse / a horse to ride is freedom of movement / a way to travel unshackled/ an old horse is a friend to confide secrets in, to trust / a strong horse can pull a plow & put dinner on a table / a team of horses can provide even more biscuits / a battalion of horses can expand borders / a horse in battle means power—hot, sweaty, horsey power.

>But this horse! / This horse is in pieces! / Someone raised this foal / someone taught it to take a harness & saddle / & the weight of a rider / & it was ridden / a soldier's companion in dark & fearful moments / when the enemy withheld in silence. / This horse is hollowed / Homer's hideout / for an opposing army.

Rigor mortis has frozen it upside down / running three-legged in the dirty grey smoke-cast sky / as if it doesn't need its fourth / now protruding somehow from its opened ribcage / to get to heaven / with its rider / possibly suffocating beneath it / & his eyes might be turned heavenward too / Elijah holding the sun.

George Yatchisin
LEAP YEAR

When Sister Patricia showed up at our door, I was sent across the street to the Puglias, which was fine by me, given nuns weren't there to be your friend. They married Jesus who was centuries dead, so you figured they couldn't be happy with that. The long game made no sense at seven-years-old, let alone the afterlife, and my atheistic future was beyond my comprehension. I don't remember what my friend Dennis and I did while my parents and the principal of St. Rose had a chat; we couldn't have even tossed a Nerf football, as they hadn't been invented yet. Computers were for NASA. TV was three networks and the remote was whoever was the youngest child in the family forced to fiddle with the controls. How lucky we were *The Brady Bunch*, *Nanny and the Professor*, and *The Partridge Family* all aired by 9 pm on ABC each Friday.

Next thing I knew, I was back home and told I was skipping second grade, as if I hit a chute on a board game sliding me faster into the future. Might have been the last thing my parents agreed on, at least about me, before they split. As if the future didn't fall like a body shot.

SWEATY PALMS

Titles and names elude me. I can quote a poem from head to tail and not remember what it's called, or a passage of scripture and forget chapter and verse. Sometimes it takes me weeks to figure out the title of a poem I finished long before. And even when I get the title, it feels like something I settled for. I meet someone the third time, the fourth time, and their name is still lost in a fog of approximations—something beginning with J or G, a name like a sluicing of water, a stormy day. But that rain doesn't feed my memory, raise up any flower of recollection, though I remember they like paratha and jogging through the park. Though I know they hum to themselves as they walk. Though I notice the flaw in the rug pattern, right where the leaf blade curves into the sundial, I can't find my glasses sitting on the desk where I placed them an hour ago, next to a book on the history of religious freedom in America which is silent about the troops of Fort Sill ending the Sun Dance by order of the government. I find what's hidden and miss what's revealed. Conceal my birthday gift, and I'll find it by dinner. Put it on the kitchen table, and I won't notice it for a month. And the gift of my days and years, are their moments slipping through the cracks in my steady gaze? Am I missing the joy of my child's smile, the beauty of my wife's subtle gestures because they're too near?—the lens of my vision bending light around all they ever meant to me until they vanish like cards in a magic trick? Must I keep my wife at arm's length to be sure I can take her all in, can take the measure of her and love her to the full before I lose sight of the pet names we once called each other, and the hand I refused to stop holding even as we fell asleep with our palms sweaty in the summer heat?

QUOTING BLAKE TO MOTHER

If I'm told to remove an epigraph from a poem, to let it stand on its own, I hear John Donne whispering in my ear, telling me a sermon about the beauty of echoes, and how our words bouncing through the hollows they travel in a landscape return to us enriched. I see a repetition of doors diminishing in size, until the smallest is one only my cat can slip through and return purring, an engine amplified to a voice saying someone said that someone said this before, in a fashion that means something like this but not this: for this is a pool, not a lake, that is a cairn but not a mountain, a mound high as the mellifluous clouds cluttered with birds hidden in their creases, and then released like a downpour. A refreshment to which someone else says, "why keep those birds there? Why let them hang in the drifting whiteness when there's nowhere to perch?" But I remember quoting Blake to Mother because she was crying, told her what Blake said about tears becoming infants in eternity and her smiling, because the quote soothed the raging waters and connected us by collapsing history into the single light of his words, and other words like them warm us in the knitted fabrics of their stories and language, scarves we can hold onto and follow all the way back to Herodotus and Hesiod and Solomon and David, their cadences dressing us against the darkness and the cold, their words assuring with an embrace, like a loving uncle who slips a coin in our pocket as we leave, so we have enough to pay for the long passage of just how far we've come.

CONTRIBUTOR NOTES

Valerie Bacharach's *Last Glimpse*, will be published by Broadstone Books, and her chapbook *After/Life* will be published by Finishing Line Press. Her poem "Birthday Portrait, Son," published by the *Ilanot Review*, was selected for inclusion in *2023 Best Small Fictions*. Her poem "Shavli" has been nominated for Best of the Net 2023 and a Pushcart Prize by *Minyan Magazine*. Her poem "Deadbolt" has been nominated for a Pushcart Prize by *RockPaperPoem*.

Ujjvala Bagal Rahn's *Red Silk Sari* (Red Silk Press, 2013) is her first collection of poems. Her work has most recently appeared in *The Threepenny Review, Illuminations, Möbius: The Journal of Social Justice, The Future Fire*, and *Bangalore Review*. She is the owner of Red Silk Press, a micropress of science fiction, science, poetry, and memoir. She lives in Savannah, GA.

Ned Balbo's newest books are *The Cylburn Touch-Me-Nots* (New Criterion Poetry Prize), and *3 Nights of the Perseids* (Richard Wilbur Award). His third book, *The Trials of Edgar Poe and Other Poems*, received the Donald Justice Prize and the 2012 Poets' Prize. A former faculty member in Iowa State University's MFA program in creative writing and environment, he has received grants from the NEA (translation) and the Maryland Arts Council. He is married to poet Jane Satterfield.

Madeleine Barnes is a writer, visual artist, and PhD candidate in the Department of English at the CUNY Graduate Center. Her debut full-length poetry collection, *You Do Not Have To Be Good*, was published by Trio House Press (2020). She is also the author of *The Memory Dictionary, Women's Work, Light Experiments*, and *The Mark My Body Draws in Light*. She's received fellowships from The Morgan Library and Museum, the PublicsLab at the Graduate Center, and the Center for Book Arts. She serves as editor-at-large at Cordella Press.

Michelle Bonczek Evory is the author of *The Ghosts of Lost Animals*, winner of the Barry Spacks Award and a 2021 Independent Publisher Book Award, as well as the open-source textbook *Naming the Unnamable: An Approach to Poetry for New Generations*. She holds a PhD in English from Western Michigan University, an MFA from Eastern Washington University, and is a creative writing mentor at The Poet's Billow, a nonprofit organization she founded with her husband poet Robert Evory.

Phillip Border received his BA in Literature from Frostburg State University, where he served as chief editor for Bittersweet. He earned his MFA from Carlow University, where he served as the inaugural emcee for the MFA Alumni Reading Series, *Raising Our Voices*. His published works have appeared in *The Amistad*, *Coal Hill Review*, *BackBone Mountain Review*, and other journals. He is the two-time recipient of The Allegany Arts Council Award for best poetry.

Rick Campbell is a poet and essayist living on Alligator Point, Florida. His most recent book is a collection of essays, *Sometimes the Light* (Main Street Rag). Poetry collections include: *Provenance* (Blue Horse Press); *Gunshot, Peacock, Dog* (Madville Publishing); *The History of Steel* (All Nations Press); *Dixmont* (Autumn House Press); *Setting the World in Order* (Texas Tech UP); *The Traveler's Companion* (Black Bay Books); and *A Day's Work* (State Street Press). His poems and essays have appeared in many journals and anthologies, including *The Georgia Review*, *Fourth River*, *Kestrel*, *Alabama Literary Review*, and *Prairie Schooner*. He's won a Pushcart Prize and an NEA Fellowship in Poetry. He teaches in the University of Nevada-Reno's MFA program.

Joseph J. Capista is the author of *Intrusive Beauty* (Ohio University Press, 2019), selected by Beth Ann Fennelly for the Hollis Summers Poetry Prize. The recipient of awards from the National Endowment for the Humanities, the Maryland State Arts Council, the Sewanee Writers' Conference, and the Bread Loaf Writers' Conference, his poems have appeared in *AGNI*, *The Georgia Review*, *The Hudson Review*, and *Ploughshares*. He holds an MFA from Warren Wilson College, teaches at Towson University, and lives with his family in Baltimore.

Gary Ciocco teaches Philosophy at several schools in the Pittsburgh/West Virginia area, and also online. He has published poetry in *Backbone Mountain Review* and *Seminary Ridge Review*, as well part of the Poet-Tree Project created by the Center for Literary Arts at

Frostburg University; this Project put poems about trees on plaques in various spots in Allegany County, MD.

TS Coody is finishing up her MFA at Texas State University, and working on her thesis manuscript currently titled *Mad Honey*.

Curtis L. Crisler was born and raised in Gary, Indiana. An award-winning poet/ author, he has six poetry books, two YA books, and five poetry chapbooks. He's been published in a variety of magazines, journals, and anthologies. He also founded the Indiana Chitlin Circuit. He is Professor of English at Purdue University Fort Wayne.

Jim Daniels's latest books include *Gun/Shy*, Wayne State University Press, a chapbook, *The Human Engine at Dawn*, Wolfson Press, and *The Luck of the Fall*, fiction, Michigan State University Press. A native of Detroit, he lives in Pittsburgh and teaches in the Alma College low-residency MFA program.

Anthony DiMatteo, poet, scholar and translator, has been secretly defending art and literature while disguised as an English professor for over thirty years at the New York Institute of Technology. His poems have recently appeared in the *American Journal of Poetry*, *Cimarron Review*, *North Dakota Quarterly* and *The MacGuffin*. His books include *Beautiful Problems*, *In Defense of Puppets*, *Secret Offices* and a recent chapbook *Fishing for Family*. He lives on the Outer Banks with his wife Kathleen O'Sullivan, pianist, designer and fellow empty nester.

Gary Fincke's collections of poetry have won what is now the Wheeler Prize (Ohio State), the Wheelbarrow Book Prize (Michigan State), the Arkansas Poetry Prize, The Jacar Press Poetry Prize, and the Stephen F. Austin Poetry Prize. Individual poems have appeared in such places as *Harper's*, *Poetry*, *The Paris Review*, *The Georgia Review*, and *The Missouri Review*.

Jeff Friedman's tenth book, *Ashes in Paradise*, was published by Madhat Press in fall 2023. Dzvinia Orlowsky's and his translation of *Memorials* by Polish Poet Mieczslaw Jastrun was published in August 2014. Nati Zohar and Friedman's book of translations *Two Gardens: Modern*

Hebrew Poems of the Bible, was published in 2016. Friedman and noted flash fiction writer Meg Pokrass have co-written a collection of fabulist microfiction, *House of Grana Padano*, published in April 2022.

Molly Fuller is the author of *For Girls Forged by Lightning: Prose & Other Poems* and *Always a Body* (forthcoming); two chapbooks *Tender the Body* and *The Neighborhood Psycho Dreams of Love*. She won the Gris-Gris Literary Magazine Summer 2020 Poetry Contest. Find her on Instagram and twitter @mollyfulleryeah.

Joy Gaines-Friedler is the author of three books of poetry, her most recent, *Capture Theory* (Kelsay Books, 2018) is a Forward Review Indiefab Finalist, and an Edward Hoffer Award, Finalist. A Best of The Net & multiple Pushcart Prize nominee, her work is published in over 80 anthologies & literary magazines. Her chapbook *Stone On Your Stone* is a 2021 winner of The Friends of Poetry, Celery City Chapbook Contest. Joy teaches Creative Writing in private workshops & for non-profits.

George Guida is the author of ten books, including five collections of poems, most recently *Zen of Pop* (Long Sky Media, 2020) and the revised edition of *New York and Other Lovers* (Encircle Publications, 2020); and novels *The Uniform* (Guernica Editions, 2024), *Posts from Suburbia*, and *The Pope Stories and Other Tales of Troubled Times*. He teaches writing and literature, at New York City College of Technology, and curates the Finger Lakes Arts Series in Dansville, New York.

Luke Hankins is the author of two full-length poetry collections, *Radiant Obstacles* and *Weak Devotions*, and a chapbook, *Testament* (Texas Review Press, 2023). His also the author of a collection of essays, *The Work of Creation*, and a volume of his translations from the French of Stella Vinitchi Radulescu, *A Cry in the Snow & Other Poems*, was released by Seagull Books. Hankins is the founder and editor of Orison Books, a non-profit literary press.

Gretchen Heyer grew up as the child of Christian missionaries in countries of Africa. Her poems can be found in *Concho River Review*, *Juked* and *Adanna*. She serves as a poetry reader for *Adroit* and works as a Jungian psychoanalyst. Her clinical and literary essays have appeared in *The Florida Review*, *Compass Rose*, *Psychoanalytic Perspectives*, and *The Journal of Analytical Psychology*.

JP Howard was the Spring 2023 Brooklyn College Tow Mentor-in-Residence. Her debut poetry collection, *SAY/MIRROR*, was a Lambda Literary finalist. She is also the author of *bury your love poems here*, *Praise This Complicated Herstory: Legacy, Healing & Revolutionary Poems* and co-edited *Sinister Wisdom Journal Black Lesbians—We Are the Revolution!* JP has received fellowships from Cave Canem, VONA, and Lambda Literary Foundation.

Tom C. Hunley has published poems in twenty-one anthologies and textbooks including *Imaginative Writing: The Elements of Craft*; *How to Write a Form Poem*; *The Inspired Poet: Writing Exercises to Spark New Work*; *Eclectica:dikter utmed vägen mellan Atlanten och Stilla Havet* (Swedish-language translations of American Poetry); and *Composing Poetry: A Guide to Writing Poems and Thinking Lyrically*.

Anna K. Jacobson is a poet, storyteller, and high school English teacher and that rare creature, a third generation Florida native. Her work has been published with *Word Revolt*, *Boned*, and in the anthologies *Moss Gossamer* and *Roots and Branches by Women Writing for (a) Change*. Her storytelling has been featured on the *Untold Stories* podcast and the *Women's Arts Collective*. Jacobson likes to describe herself in the words of her favorite fictional detective, Lord Peter Wimsey, as getting 'so easily drunk on words that she is seldom sober."

Peter Johnson's poetry and fiction have received fellowships from the National Endowment for the Arts and Rhode Island Council on the Arts, and his second book of prose poems was awarded the James Laughlin Award from the Academy of American Poets. His most recent book is *While the Undertaker Sleeps: Collected and New Prose Poems*.

Richard Jordan is a Ph.D. mathematician who also writes poetry. His poems have appeared or are forthcoming in *Rattle* (finalist in the 2022 Rattle Poetry Prize competition), *Valparaiso Poetry Review*, *New York Quarterly*, *Tar River Poetry*, *The Atlanta Review*, *Kestrel*, *The National*

Poetry Review, Little Patuxent Review, and elsewhere. He resides in the Boston area.

Elizabeth Kerlikowske is the author of *The Vaudeville Horse* (2022, Etchings Press) a collection of prose poems. Her book before that was *Art Speaks*, an ekphrastic text with painter Mary Hatch. She works for two poetry nonprofits and was awarded the Community Medal for the Arts (Kalamazoo) in 2017. She volunteers at an alternative high school.

Nina Kossman, a Jewish refugee from the former Soviet Union, is a bilingual poet, memoirist, playwright, short story writer, novelist, and artist. She has authored, edited, or edited and translated nine books of poetry and prose. She is a recipient of several awards and fellowships, including an NEA fellowship, and grants from the Foundation for Hellenic Culture, the Onassis Public Benefit Foundation and Fundación Valparaíso.

Jennifer Kwon Dobbs is the author of *Interrogation Room*, winner of the Association of Asian American Studies Award in Poetry, and *Paper Pavilion*, which won the White Pine Press Poetry Prize; and the chapbooks *Notes from a Missing Person* and *Necro Citizens*. Her co-translation of Sámi poet Niillas Holmberg's *Juolgevuođđu*, published as *Underfoot*, received the American-Scandinavian Foundation's Lief and Inger Sjöberg Prize. She is senior poetry editor of *AGNI* and professor of English at St. Olaf College.

Gerry LaFemina's most recent books are *After the War for Independence* (poems) and *The Pursuit: A Meditation on Happiness* (creative nonfiction). A noted arts activist he is a Professor of English at Frostburg State University, serves as a Mentor in the MFA Program at Carlow University, and is a current Fulbright Specialist in Writing, Literature, and American Culture. He also edited this anthology.

Laura Last is a singer and poet living in the Hudson Valley. Her poems have appeared in the *Laurel Review* and elsewhere, and she has received support for her work from the Tucson Festival of Books. She is pursuing her MFA in Poetry and Literature at the Bennington Writers Seminar.

Joseph Lerner's fiction and poetry have appeared in *100 WordStory, Alternate Route, BlazeVOX, Gargoyle, matchbook, Mojave River Review,* and elsewhere. In 1981 he founded, as editor/publisher, *The Washington (DC) Book Review* and, in 1992, *Furious Fictions, A Magazine of Short-Short Stories,* one of the first literary journals devoted exclusively to flash fiction.

Geri Lipschultz's recent stories in *BigCityLit* and *Orca* received Pushcart nominations. Otherwise, her publications include work in *Terrain, The Rumpus, Ms., New York Times, Black Warrior Review,* and *College English* among others. Geri teaches writing at Hunter College and Borough of Manhattan Community College. She was awarded a Creative Artists in Public Service (CAPS) grant from New York State for her fiction.

Lorette C. Luzajic reads, writes, publishes, edits, and teaches flash fiction and prose poetry. Her own have appeared in numerous journals and anthologies. She is also the author of two collections, *Pretty Time Machine* and *Winter in June,* and two upcoming books, *The Neon Rosary: tiny ekphrastic prose poems,* and *The Rope Artist: ekphrastic small fictions.* Lorette is the founding editor of *The Ekphrastic Review,* and is also an award-winning neoexpressionist artist, with collectors in more than 30 countries so far.

Gary McDowell is the author of *Aflame,* winner of the 2019 White Pine Press Poetry Prize. His other books include *Caesura: Essays; Mysteries in a World that Thinks There Are None,* winner of the 2014 Burnside Review Book Award; *Weeping at a Stranger's Funeral;* and *American Amen,* winner of the 2009 Orphic Prize for Poetry. He is also the co-editor of *The Rose Metal Press Field Guide to Prose Poetry: Contemporary Poets in Discussion and Practice.* He lives in Nashville, TN where he is Professor of English and Director of the MFA Program at Belmont University.

Kathleen McGookey has published four books of prose poems and three chapbooks, most recently *Instructions for My Imposter* (Press 53) and *Nineteen Letters* (BatCat Press). She has also published *We'll See,* a book of translations of French poet Georges Godeau's prose poems. Her work has appeared in journals including *Copper Nickel*, *Field*, *Ploughshares*, *Prairie Schooner*, and *The Southern Review*, and was featured on American Life in Poetry. She has received grants from the French Ministry of Foreign Affairs and the Sustainable Arts Foundation.

Jennifer Militello is the author of the poetry collection *The Pact* (Tupelo Press/Shearsman Books, 2021) and the memoir *Knock Wood*, winner of the Dzanc Nonfiction Award, as well as four additional collections of poetry. Her work has appeared in *Best American Poetry*, *Best New Poets*, *American Poetry Review*, *The Nation*, *The New Republic*, *The Paris Review*, *POETRY*, and *Tin House*.

Robert Miltner's books include a collection of flash nonfiction, *Ohio Apertures* (Cornerstone Press, 2021); a collection of short stories, *And Your Bird Can Sing*; and three collections of prose poetry: *Hotel Utopia*, *Orpheus & Echo*, and the forth-coming *Cicatrix Vortex Codex*. He is professor emeritus from Kent State University Stark and the NEOMFA.

Erin Murphy's ninth book of poems, *Human Resources*, is forthcoming from Salmon Poetry. Her awards include *The Rattle* Poetry Prize Reader's Choice Award, The Normal School Poetry Prize, the Dorothy Sargent Rosenberg Poetry Prize, and a Best of the Net award. She is editor of three anthologies from the University of Nebraska Press and SUNY Press and serves as Poetry Editor of *The Summerset Review*. She is Professor of English at Penn State Altoona.

Kerry Neville is the author of two collections of stories, *Necessary Lies*, which received the G. S. Sharat Chandra Prize in Fiction, and *Remember to Forget Me*. In 2018, she was a Fulbright Fellow at University of Limerick in Ireland, where she was Visiting Faculty in the MA in Creative Writing Program and continues as faculty in the Frank McCourt/University of Limerick Summer Writing School. She is an Associate Professor and Coordinator of the MFA and Undergraduate Creative Writing Program at Georgia College and State University.

Robert Perchan's latest books are the comic novella *Tropic of Scorpio* (Spuyten Duyvil Press, 2022) and *Last Notes from a Split Peninsula: Poems and Prose Poems*. His collection *Fluid in Darkness, Frozen* *in Light* won the 1999 Pearl Poetry Prize. He also has two poetry chapbooks to his credit as well as the avant-la-lettre flash novella *Perchan's Chorea: Eros and Exile*. He continues to eat and drink in Busan, South Korea, under the bemused gaze of his translator wife, Mi-kyung Lee.

Ruben Quesada is the editor *Latinx Poetics: Essays on the Art of Poetry*, and author of *Jane: La Segua, Revelations*, and *Next Extinct Mammal*. His writing appears in the *New York Times, Best American Poetry, American Poetry Review, Pleiades, Harvard Review*, and elsewhere. He teaches in the MFA Program in Creative Writing at Antioch University-Los Angeles.

Christine Rhein is the author of *Wild Flight*, a winner of the Walt McDonald Poetry Book Prize (Texas Tech University Press). Her poems have appeared in journals such as *The Southern Review, The Gettysburg Review, Michigan Quarterly Review*, and *Rattle*, and have been selected for Poetry Daily, Verse Daily, and anthologies including *Best New Poets* and *The Best American Nonrequired Reading*. A former automotive engineer, she lives in Brighton, Michigan.

Lee Ann Roripaugh is a biracial Nisei and the author of five volumes of poetry, mostly recently *tsunami vs. the fukushima 50* (Milkweed Editions, 2019), which was named a "Best Book of 2019" by the New York Public Library, selected as a poetry Finalist in the 2020 Lambda Literary Awards, and was named one of the "50 Must-Read Poetry Collections in 2019" by *Book Riot*. Her collection, *Reveal Codes*, was selected as winner of the Moon City Press Short Fiction Award and published in late 2023, and her chapbook, *#stringofbeads*, a winner in the Diode Editions Chapbook Competition, was released in 2023.

Jane Satterfield has published five poetry books, including *The Badass Brontës*, a winner of the Diode Editions Poetry Prize, *Apocalypse Mix*, and *Assignation at Vanishing Point*. She is the recipient of a National Endowment for the Arts poetry fellowship, the 49th Parallel Award for Poetry from Bellingham Review, the Ledbury Poetry Festival Prize, and more. She is married to poet Ned Balbo and lives in Baltimore, where she is a professor of writing at Loyola University Maryland.

Katherine Smith's recent poetry publications include appearances in *Boulevard, North American Review, Ploughshares, Cincinnati Review, Missouri Review*, and other journals. Her books are *Argument by Design, Woman Alone on the Mountain*, and most recently *Secret City*, (Madville, 2022). She works at Montgomery College in Maryland where she is poetry editor of the Potomac Review.

Joshua Michael Stewart is the author of three poetry collections: *Break Every String, The Bastard Children of Dharma Bums*, and *Love Something*. His poems have appeared in the *Massachusetts Review, Salamander, Plainsongs, South Dakota Review, Permafrost*, and many others. He lives in Ware, Massachusetts.

Virgil Suárez was born in Cuba. He is the author of a multitude of books, most recently *Amerikan Chernobyl*. He lives in Fucked Up Florida.

Matthew Thorburn's most recent book is *String* (Louisiana State University Press, 2023). He's also the author of seven previous collections of poetry, including *The Grace of Distance*, a finalist for the Paterson Poetry Prize, and *Dear Almost*, which received the Lascaux Prize. His work has been recognized with a Witter Bynner Fellowship from the Library of Congress, as well as fellowships from the Bronx and New Jersey arts councils. He lives with his family in New Jersey.

Eric Torgersen has published eight books and chapbooks of poetry, two of fiction, and a full-length study of Rainer Maria Rilke and Paula Modersohn-Becker. He also translates German poetry, especially that of Rainer Maria Rilke and Nicolas Born. After two years in the Peace Corps in Ethiopia, he earned an MFA in poetry from the University of Iowa. He lives in Mt. Pleasant, Michigan with his wife, the quilt artist Ann Kowaleski.

Pat Valdata is a poet and novelist. Her book about women aviation pioneers, *Where No Man Can Touch*, won the 2015 Donald Justice Poetry Prize and was published in a revised edition in 2023. Her poetry has appeared in *Ecotone, Ekphrastic Review, Italian Americana, North*

American Review, and others. In 2021 she received an individual artist award from the Maryland State Arts Council. Pat lives in Crisfield, Maryland, with her husband and their rescue poodle, Junior.

Doug Van Gundy directs the Low-Residency MFA program in Creative Writing at West Virginia Wesleyan College. His poem and essays have appeared in many journals, including *Poets & Writers*, *Poetry* and *The Oxford American*. He is the author of a book of poems, *A Life Above Water* and co-editor of the anthology *Eyes Glowing at the Edge of the Woods: Contemporary Writing from West Virginia*. His second collection is forthcoming from The University Press of Kentucky.

Elinor Ann Walker holds a Ph.D. in English from the University of North Carolina-Chapel Hill, lives with her husband and two dogs near the mountains, and prefers to write outside. She teaches remotely for University of Maryland Global Campus. Her recent poetry, flash fiction, and creative non-fiction are featured or forthcoming in *Cherry Tree*, *Hayden's Ferry Review*, *Jet Fuel Review*, *Nimrod International Journal*, *Northwest Review*, *Plume*, *The Southern Review*, and elsewhere.

Greg Watson's work has appeared in numerous literary journals and anthologies. He is the author of nine collections of poetry, most recently *The Sound of Light*. He is also co-editor with Richard Broderick of *The Road by Heart: Poems of Fatherhood*, published by Nodin Press.

Cathy Wittmeyer hosts the Word to Action poetry retreat in the Alps where poets unearth connections between climate wreckage and human frailty. Editor of the upcoming anthology: *Eden is a Backyard: Climate poems from Word to Action* from Edition Eupolinos, her work has appeared in various journals and her poem won an Honorable Mention in the 1982 SPCA poster contest.

George Yatchisin is the author of *Feast Days* and *The First Night We Thought the World Would End* (Brandenburg Press 2019). His poems have been published in journals including *Antioch Review*, *Askew*, and *Zocalo Public Square*. He is co-editor of the anthology *Rare Feathers: Poems on Birds & Art*, and his poetry appears in anthologies including *Reel Verse: Poems About the Movies*.

Michael T. Young's third full-length collection, *The Infinite Doctrine of Water*, was longlisted for the Julie Suk Award. He received a Fellowship from the New Jersey State Council on the Arts and the Jean Pedrick Chapbook Award for his collection, *Living in the Counterpoint*. His poetry has been featured on Verse Daily and The Writer's Almanac. It has also appeared in numerous journals including *OneArt, Pinyon, Talking River Review,* and *Valparaiso Poetry Review*.

ACKNOWLEDGMENTS

All rights reserved. Each of these poems is used with permission of its author.

"Parable of the Forest Pygmy" and "Forgetting the Nicene Creed" by Rick Campbell first appeared in *Provenance* (2020, Blue Horse Press).

"The Story of a Life," by George Guida, first appeared in *Philadelphia Poets* (2019).

"Vaccination in the Broadest Sense of the Term," "Crickets" and "Nice Socks" by Peter Johnson first appeared in *Plume Poetry*.

"Jesus on the River" by Richard Jordan first appeared in *Unbroken: Prose Poems*. "Mackerel Day" by Richard Jordan first appeared in *Sugar House Review*. "With Feathers" by Richard Jordan first appeared in *Arboreal Literary Magazine*.

"Tabula Rasa" by Elizabeth Kerlikowske first appeared in *Cloudbank*.

"Fantastic Imaginary Creatures" by Gerry LaFemina first appeared in *Pithead Chapel*.

"The Cell" and "To Gabriela, In Memory" by Ruben Quesada first appeared in *Next Extinct Mammal* (Greenhouse Review Press, 2011).

"Notes on Dissociation" by Lee Ann Roripaugh first appeared in *Sweet Literary*.

"Latin 121" by Jane Satterfield first appeared in *Her Familiars* (2013, Elixir Press).

"Mayfly" by Pat Valdata first appeared in *Where No Man Can Touch* (2023, Wind Canyon Books). All rights reserved. Used with permission of author.

"Object Impermanence" by Elinor Ann Walker first appeared in *Hayden's Ferry Review*. "Fugue State" by Elinor Ann Walker first appeared in *Jet Fuel Review*.

Printed in the USA
CPSIA information can be obtained
at www.ICGtesting.com
JSHW021142240324
59625JS00003B/40